PRAISE FOR *MOMENTUM*

This book is at once delightful, convicting, and practical. *Delightful*, because it is so well written with excellent illustrations; *convicting*, in that it aims at the transformation of our hearts; and finally, *practical*, because it spell out exactly what we can do to gain the momentum in the Christian life that we all seek. What you hold in your hand is a treasure that helps us understand the Beatitudes and that motivates us to become what Jesus redeemed us to be. Read it and you will want to share it with a friend!

ERWIN W. LUTZER
Pastor Emeritus, The Moody Church, Chicago

Without fail, my mind, heart, and walk with God are always stirred by Colin Smith's messages. Solid biblical exposition, heart-searching insight, and practical exhortation make this study of the Beatitudes a rich resource.

NANCY DeMOSS WOLGEMUTH
Author, Revive Our Hearts teacher and host

I have never before thought of the progression in Jesus' Beatitudes. And I'll never read them the same way again after Colin Smith's insightful book, *Momentum*. From the poor in spirit to the persecuted for righteousness' sake, Christians all along the sanctification spectrum will be edified by this wise work.

COLLIN HANSEN
Editorial Director, The Gospel Coalition
Author, *Blind Spots: Becoming a Courageous, Compassionate, and Commissioned Church*

The Christian understanding of blessing has been greatly watered down to represent a few shallow aspects at the cost of the rich biblical connotations that go with it. Colin Smith redresses this with a deep, enriching exposition. Usually when I seek this kind of enrichment I go to writers of previous generations. This book has the same depth but is also written in a vibrant, contemporary style.

AJITH FERNANDO
Teaching Director, Youth for Christ, Sri Lanka

In *Momentum*, Colin Smith leaves behind our culture's superficial use of #blessed as a hashtag to brag about favorable circumstances to mine the counterintuitive wisdom of what Jesus says it really means to have a life that is blessed. This book will cause you to look deeply into your own heart and life for signs of genuine spiritual life as well as equip you to pursue more purposefully the Giver of life.

NANCY GUTHRIE
Bible teacher and author

Colin Smith's series on the *Momentum* is a soul-searching investigation into Jesus' teachings on the Beatitudes. The beauty of this study is that it asks the right questions and then it answers them in straightforward and plain English. Here is a gift that would bless many a church and many a Bible study group.

WALTER C. KAISER JR.
President Emeritus, Gordon-Conwell Theological Seminary

I love this book. Thank you Colin for the refreshing, insightful and compelling way in which you open the Beatitudes to us. Indeed, the Beatitudes are the marks and evidence of new life in Christ, as well as a practical model for growth in the Christian life. This book is for every follower of Christ who wants to get unstuck and experience momentum in their walk with Christ. What a gift!

CRAWFORD W. LORITTS JR.
Author, Speaker, Radio Host
Senior Pastor, Fellowship Bible Church, Roswell, Georgia

MOMENTUM

MOMENTUM

PURSUING GOD'S BLESSINGS THROUGH THE BEATITUDES

COLIN S. SMITH

MOODY PUBLISHERS
CHICAGO

© 2016 by
COLIN S. SMITH

Published in association with the literary agency of Wolgemuth & Associates, Inc.

All websites and phone numbers listed herein are accurate at the time of publication but may change in the future or cease to exist. The listing of website references and resources does not imply publisher endorsement of the site's entire contents.

Edited by Jim Vincent
Author photo: Melissa Marie Photography
Cover and Interior design: Erik M. Peterson
Cover image of gymnast © Celso Diniz / Dreamstime.com (36731508)

Library of Congress Cataloging-in-Publication Data

Names: Smith, Colin S., 1958- author.
Title: Momentum : practicing the beatitudes to overcome sin and pursue God's
   blessing / Colin S. Smith.
Description: Chicago : Moody Publishers, 2016. | Includes bibliographical
   references.
Identifiers: LCCN 2016029381 (print) | LCCN 2016031888 (ebook) | ISBN
   9780802413864 | ISBN 9780802493743 ()
Subjects: LCSH: Beatitudes--Criticism, interpretation, etc.
Classification: LCC BT382 .S623 2016 (print) | LCC BT382 (ebook) | DDC
   226.9/306--dc23
LC record available at https://lccn.loc.gov/2016029381

ISBN: 978-0-8024-1386-4

We hope you enjoy this book from Moody Publishers. Our goal is to provide high-quality, thought-provoking books and products that connect truth to your real needs and challenges. For more information on other books and products written and produced from a biblical perspective, go to www.moodypublishers.com or write to:

Moody Publishers
820 N. LaSalle Boulevard
Chicago, IL 60610

1 3 5 7 9 10 8 6 4 2

Printed in the United States of America

To Charlie and Mary Lou Hess
and Jon and Kim Swisher,
with whom we share the joy
of children walking in the truth.

CONTENTS

INTRODUCTION

GAINING MOMENTUM

So you want to know more of God's blessings in your life.
Me too.

The sad reality is that many who profess to be Christians get stuck. They settle for the little that they have, and reconcile themselves to remaining as they are.

But not you. Somewhere deep in your heart there is a longing for more. You want to live under the blessing of God. You want to enjoy His smile and His favor. You want to be able to say with David that your cup overflows.

But you face some serious challenges. What does a blessed life look like? How do you move in that direction? Where do you begin? And what can you do about all the stuff that gets in the way?

Everyone wants to be blessed. We want to be blessed in our relationships, in our businesses, and in our churches. We want to be blessed in life, death, and eternity. The opposite of being blessed is being cursed, and nobody wants that.

No one knows where blessing is to be found more than Jesus Christ, and so when He speaks about blessing, as He does in the Beatitudes (Matt. 5:1–12), I want to listen and so should you.

WHAT IS THE BLESSED LIFE?

What does a blessed life look like? Is it having a happy marriage? Gifted children? Good health? Fulfilling work? Financial stability? Opportunities to travel? Belonging to a healthy church?

All of these are rich blessings indeed, and you could add to the list, but before you do, think about this: not one of these gifts is included in our Lord's description of the life that is blessed.

Not one!

Jesus does not say, "Blessed are the happily married" but "Blessed are the poor in spirit." He does not say, "Blessed are those who enjoy good health" but "Blessed are those who mourn."

According to Jesus the greatest blessings are not found in the places where we normally look, but rather in places that, at first, we may not be inclined to explore.

The Beatitudes are counterintuitive. Being poor means that you don't have resources. Nobody wants that. But Jesus speaks of a kind of poverty that makes you rich! Mourning means that you have great sorrow, and that won't be on your wish list. But Jesus speaks of a kind of mourning that leads to joy.

HOW DO YOU RECOGNIZE A TRUE CHRISTIAN?

Our aim in this book is to make progress in the Christian life, and in order to advance, we need to have a clear understanding of the goal. What is this life in which you wish to grow? What should you pursue? What, in short, are the distinguishing marks of an authentic Christian?

Think with me for a moment about bird-watching. Birds are known by their distinguishing marks. You know an American goldfinch by its distinctive yellow color, and you know a spotted sandpiper by its long beak and distinctive spots.

But how would you know a true Christian? What are the distinguishing marks of a person who lives under the blessing of God? The starting point for making progress in the Christian life is to know for sure that you are in fact a Christian. But how would you know a true Christian if you saw one?

Someone might say, "I would know that a person is a Christian by what she believes." That's a good answer, so let's explore it. After all, God has revealed certain truths in the Scriptures, and the person who does not believe them cannot be a Christian. Jesus says, "Unless you *believe* that I am he you will die in your sins" (John 8:24, emphasis added). He also said that the work of God is to *believe* in the Father who sent His Son into the world (John 6:29). These verses, along with many more, teach us that there are certain beliefs without which a person cannot be a Christian.

But James reminds us that even the devils believe (James 2:19). Satan knows that Jesus died for sinners. He knows that Christ rose from the dead and that He is the ascended Lord of the universe. All of this is clear in the unseen world, and that is why, in the Gospels, a demon was the first to confess Jesus as "the Holy One of God" (Mark 1:24). Satan knows the truth of who Jesus is and what He has done, but refuses to submit to Him, and continues to operate as the self-crowned lord of his own life.

In the same way, you will know, as I do, people who profess Christian faith while quietly indulging the sins of their choice. Such a person is not a Christian but a hypocrite, and hypocrites do not live under the blessing of God. There's more to being a Christian than knowing the truth. Believing is a necessary mark, but it is not sufficient to identify a genuine Christian.

Are there any other ways to spot a real Christian? Someone else might say, "I would know that a person is a Christian by what they do. It's not words but deeds that count." Again, this is a good answer. Jesus said, "Everyone who hears these words of mine *and does them will be* like a wise man who built his house on the rock" (Matt. 7:24, emphasis added). But our Lord also speaks of people who work in His name to whom, on the last day, He will say, "I never knew you; depart from me" (Matt. 7:23). Here are people who were active in ministry but they were not true Christians.

It seems from the words of Jesus that these people will be taken by surprise at this announcement. Some of them could point to the work they did in teaching the Bible, confronting evil in society, or bringing change that was for the good of many people. These are impressive works, but according to Jesus, none of them, in themselves, give conclusive evidence that a person belongs to Christ.

So to make this personal, on the last day there would be no value in me saying to Jesus, "I was the senior pastor of a large church outside Chicago!" That is not what He is looking for. The blessing of God is not found through having a position in ministry any more than it is found through assenting to all the doctrines of the Christian faith. What you do for Jesus, however impressive, does not, in itself, demonstrate that you are a Christian.

When our Lord sits down with His disciples to tell them about life under the blessing of God, He does not begin with a class on doctrine or with a mandate for mission. Instead, He describes a person who is poor in spirit, mourns over his or her sins, meekly submits to the will of God, and so longs to grow in righteousness. It is in the life of such a person that the blessing of God is to be found.

ASKING SOME HONEST QUESTIONS

So I invite you to open your heart with me to the searching gaze of Jesus, to examine your interior life, and to discern your spiritual condition. Are the distinguishing marks of a life under the blessing of God evident in you?

Ask yourself some honest questions:

"Blessed are the peacemakers" (Matt. 5:9). Am I a person who brings

peace? Does peace follow me because it lives in me? Or do other people at home or in the workplace experience tension *from* me because of the turmoil that is *in* me?

"Blessed are the pure in heart" (v. 8). What is the condition of my heart? To what extent has my inner life been fouled up by impurity?

"Blessed are the merciful" (v. 7). How am I doing when it comes to this business of forgiving others? Do I forgive quickly? Am I merciful toward the weaknesses of others who have failed me?

When Jesus describes the person who is blessed, is He describing you? This is searching stuff. It cuts through the shallowness and cheap talk that too often fills our churches.

The church at its best is a mixed bag of genuine Christians and people who have deceived themselves over their true spiritual condition. A person who rests on a vacuous decision made years ago, which has had little or no effect on his or her life, desperately needs to hear the wake-up call that rings out from these words of Jesus.

STANDING IN GRACE AND STRIVING FOR GROWTH

Before we go further, I need to pause and make one thing crystal clear. The Beatitudes tell you what a true Christian looks like. They do not describe the process by which a person becomes a Christian.

The goldfinch is known by its distinctive yellow color, but the yellow color did not make the bird a goldfinch. The bird is yellow because it is a goldfinch. Its nature gives rise to its color, and its color reflects its nature. Painting yellow dye on a blackbird would not make it a goldfinch.

This distinction is really important when it comes to rightly understanding the teaching of Jesus in the Beatitudes. A Christian is known by the distinguishing marks set out by Jesus. But these marks are the evidence of new life in Christ, not its cause.

The message of Jesus is not, "If you humble yourself and mourn over your sins and submit yourself meekly to God and get an appetite for righteousness, God will smile on you and you will get into heaven." That would be salvation by works and that is not the teaching of the Bible.

The smile of God's favor is yours when, through the bond of faith, Christ becomes yours and you become His. Being "in Christ" brings you into an entirely new position before God, in which He cleanses you from your sins, removing them from you so completely that they cannot be charged against you either now or in the future (Rom. 5:1; 8:1; Eph. 1:3–7). He reconciles you to the Father, transforming your relationship with God from that of a sinner facing impending judgment to that of a son or daughter anticipating a glorious inheritance. And He breathes His Holy Spirit into you, filling you with the power and presence of His own life. That changes your nature, and this is where the Christian life begins. Being justified by faith in the Lord Jesus Christ, we have "peace with God" and "access by faith into this grace in which we stand" (Rom. 5:1–2).

Standing in grace is really good news. Grace is not a stepping-stone on which we rest for a moment in order to move on to something else. It is where we stand at the beginning of the Christian life and where we remain until its end. Anything less would leave us as lost as we would have been if Jesus Christ had never come into the world. Suppose, for example, that God were to blot out all your sins, hand you a clean slate, and then say to you, "Don't mess up again!" What chance would you have of success? None whatsoever. The root of sin remains in you, and you will be as dependent on the grace of God on your last day as a Christian as you were on your first.

The good news is that, being justified by faith, you have access to grace in which you *stand*, because of Jesus Christ and all that He has done for you in His life, death, and resurrection, and all that He continues to do for you as your advocate and intercessor at the right hand of the Father.

A Christian is a person who stands in grace, but standing in grace and striving for growth belong together in the same way as a goldfinch and that distinctive yellow color are inseparable.

Thomas Watson (ca. 1620–86) wrote a book called *The Beatitudes*, which, to my mind, is the most helpful work ever written on this part of the Bible. He had an extraordinary gift for saying profound things in memorable sentences, and we will draw from his wisdom often in this book.

Watson says, "If we do not imitate His [Christ's] life, we cannot be saved by His death."[1] Listen carefully to what he is saying. Watson is quite clear: we are saved by Christ's death. He does *not* say that we are saved by imitating Christ's life. What he *does* say, and what more importantly the Bible makes clear, is that the distinguishing mark of a person who is saved by Christ's death is that he or she seeks to imitate Christ's life.

A person who stands in grace has a heart for holiness, and *without holiness no one will see the Lord* (Heb. 12:14). Again, our holiness is not the reason that we will enter heaven. Grace is. But the pursuit of holiness is the distinguishing mark of a person who stands in grace, and the two belong together, because they are found inseparably in Christ.

Jesus Christ "became to us wisdom from God, righteousness and sanctification and redemption" (1 Cor. 1:30). So when Christ becomes yours, you get more than righteousness. Christ is your sanctification, your wisdom, and your redemption as well. All of these gifts are in Him and He never gives one without the others.

God offers multiple blessings to us in the gospel. There's forgiveness, reconciliation, holiness, and heaven, to name just a few. But God does not offer any of these gifts in isolation. He offers all of them to us "in Christ."

Christ is the mega-gift, and He contains all the other gifts in Himself. With Him you have all of them, and without Him you have none of them. "Whoever has the Son has life; whoever does not have the Son of

God does not have life" (1 John 5:12). All of the blessings of the gospel come to you in Christ and remain with you through Him. None of them would be possible without Him.

God offers one gift to us: Jesus. He is all that we need, and we are blessed with every spiritual blessing in Christ (Eph. 1:3).

When Christ takes command of your life, He forgives your sin, changes your heart, reconciles you to the Father, adopts you into His family, and gives you His Spirit. His work is indivisible, and it is for this reason that a person who stands in grace has a heart for holiness.

So here's how you know that you are standing in grace: you start pursuing holiness. Your will has, in substantial measure, been realigned with God's will, and your great desire, mirroring His, is that you will fully reflect the beauty of Jesus, who now lives in you.

WHEN DESPAIR SEEMS NEAR

At this point, you may need a word of encouragement. If you are like me, you will find that when you look at your own life you are more aware of your failings than your successes, and more conscious of your shortcomings than your progress. So when you examine yourself in the light of the Beatitudes you will be challenged, which is good, but you may also feel overwhelmed, which would be bad.

So if you are going to be honest with yourself and open your life to the searching gaze of Christ through the Scriptures, you need to know how to handle the truth about yourself without giving way to despair.

I recently spoke with a new Christian who told me that, for all the joy she had found in Christ, she was feeling worse about herself than she did before she became a believer. Was this normal, she wondered? Was she doing something wrong?

I tried to explain to her that before she became a Christian she had been deaf to the Holy Spirit and blind to the glory of Christ. But when the Holy Spirit began His saving work in her life, He opened her ears and eyes to the truth, and so she became convicted about sin, righteousness, and judgment (John 16:8).

Being convinced of sin means you have a growing awareness of how far you fall short of the life to which God has called you. Seeing that gulf, you quickly realize that righteousness is far beyond your reach and that apart from Jesus Christ you would fall under the just condemnation of God. You may not have seen these things before, and it is only because of the work of the Holy Spirit that you are seeing and feeling them now. More than that, it is because you see these things that you cling to Christ. You know your continuing need and you find peace, hope, and joy not in an assessment of your own progress or lack of it in the Christian life, but through the grace that you have in Him.

CLINGING TIGHTLY TO CHRIST

So here's how to handle the discouragement that you may feel about your own lack of progress. Whenever you see your own need or feel your own failure, use that moment of insight to cling more tightly, more gratefully, and more joyfully to Jesus Christ and all that He has accomplished on the cross for you. And then be thankful that the reason you see your sins and failings so clearly, and even painfully, is that the Holy Spirit lives in you and that He is calling you to step forward in the path of progress. Never let your lack of progress become a reason for despair.

Some years ago, I came across a statement in the Heidelberg Catechism that has helped me get a perspective on this tension between standing in grace and striving for growth.

A catechism is a tool for teaching and learning the core truths of the Christian faith, and Heidelberg is, to my mind, one of the best. The first two sections deal with "Misery" (our fallen condition as human beings on account of sin) and "Deliverance" (God's way of rescuing His people by grace, through Jesus Christ).

The third section is entitled "Gratitude," and it deals with the response of a Christian to all that God has done for us in a life of faith and obedience. Having laid out the meaning and application of God's commandments for Christians today, the catechism asks this question:

> *Q. But can those converted to God obey these commandments*
> *perfectly?*
> *The first part of the answer is as follows;*
> *A. No.*
> *In this life even the holiest have only a small beginning of*
> *this obedience.*[2]

The holiest person you know has only a *small beginning of obedience* in this life! Wow! Test this out by talking with someone who knows what it is to walk with God, and has done so for many years. They will tell you that they are more conscious of how far they still have to go than they are of the distance they have come.

Even the holiest make only a small beginning in this life. That truth helps us. You may feel that others are light-years ahead of you in the Christian life, but the truth is that they are as much in need of God's grace right now as you are. In the light of God's holiness we are all like snails setting out on a mile-long journey, in which the best of us only travel a few feet in a lifetime and the distance between us is measured in inches.

Even the holiest person has only made a small beginning in pursuing the purity, peace, contentment, and joy that one day will be yours as much as it will be theirs.

But there's more. Having established that no Christian obeys God's law perfectly and that the best of us have only made a small beginning, the catechism goes on to say:

Nevertheless, with all seriousness of purpose they do begin to live according to all, not only some, of God's commandments.

In every Christian there really is a beginning of holiness, a beginning of purity, a beginning of contentment, a beginning of peace. Love for God and love for others, though far from complete, is truly begun in the life of every believer, and what God has begun in you He will certainly complete.

ROOT, SHOOT, AND FRUIT

Having begun, you will want to move forward, and it is here that the Beatitudes help, not only by telling us what a blessed life looks like, but by showing us how to make progress. There is a definite order in the Beatitudes, and each one flows from the others that went before. The Beatitudes do more than describe a blessed life—they give us a road map for pursuing it.

The first three beatitudes deal with our need. We are poor in spirit (Matt. 5:3) because we do not have what it takes to live as God commands. We mourn (v. 4) because our sins are many. We become meek, rather than self-willed and defiant (v. 5), because we do not have the ability to direct our own lives wisely. These are the *roots* of a blessed and godly life.

Out of these roots come the *shoots* of the fourth beatitude, a hunger and thirst for righteousness (v. 6). God uses the root of seeing your own need to produce the shoot of a deep longing to grow in righteousness. When the roots of the first three beatitudes are nourished, a great desire for righteousness will spring up in your life.

Continuing the metaphor, the roots produce shoots, and the shoots bear *fruit*. The fruit of this blessed and godly life is, first, mercy or forgiveness (v. 7), then purity (v. 8), and finally peace (v. 9).

Our Lord also gave us an eighth beatitude, "Blessed are those who

21

are persecuted" (Matt. 5:10). This one is different from the rest because the others all reflect character that God's people are actively to pursue. Persecution is different. We are not to pursue it, but we are to understand that when we go after the blessed and godly life that Jesus lays out for us in the Beatitudes, persecution will pursue us. Those who are blessed by God will be persecuted in this world.

Now think with me for a moment about this *root-shoot-fruit* pattern. It's obvious that you cannot get the fruit without the shoot, and you do not get the shoot without the root. The order is important. If you want to have the fruits of forgiveness, purity, and peace in your life, you have to begin with the roots of becoming poor in spirit, mourning over your sins, and meekly submitting yourself to the will of God. The order of the Beatitudes shows you *how to make progress* in the Christian life.

WISDOM FROM THE PAST

This is something that I learned from older writers, and when I began teaching it in the church that I serve, many people responded by saying first that they had not heard this before, and second that they found it helpful. Thoughtful Christians are rightly cautious of anything new when it comes to our understanding of the Bible.

So it is important to know that seeing order in the Beatitudes and using this pattern as a model for progress in the Christian life is well represented in the wisdom of those who have gone before.

The great nineteenth-century preacher C. H. Spurgeon (1834–92) began a series of sermons on the Beatitudes in 1873. Having introduced each of the blessings, he pointed out the importance of their order.

> Observe carefully, and you will see that *each one rises above those which precede it. . . .* There is a great advance from the poor in spirit to the pure in heart and the peacemaker.
>
> Not only do the Beatitudes rise, one above another, but they *spring out*

22

of each other, as if each depended on all that went before. Each growth feeds a higher growth, and the seventh is the product of all the other six. . . . The stones are laid one upon another . . . they are the natural sequel and completion of each other, even as were the seven days of the world's first week.[3]

Martyn Lloyd-Jones (1899–1981), one of the greatest preachers of the twentieth century, took the same position: "There is, beyond any question, a very definite order in these Beatitudes. Our Lord does not place them in their respective positions haphazardly or accidentally; there is what we may describe as a spiritual logical sequence to be found here."[4]

Alexander Maclaren (1826–1910), best known for his thirty-two volume commentary on the entire Bible, is of the same opinion: "Each Beatitude springs from the preceding, and all twined together make an ornament of grace upon the neck, a chain of jewels."[5]

Taking up the image of jewels strung together in a necklace, he says,

> An ordinary superficial view of these so-called Beatitudes is that they are simply a collection of unrelated sayings. But they are a great deal more than that. There is a vital connection and progress in them. The jewels are not flung down in a heap, they are wreathed together in a chain.[6]

This theme of progress is a really helpful insight that we will come back to repeatedly in our journey through the Beatitudes. But as with any insight, it is important not to press it too far. It would be a great mistake, for example, to imagine that you have to spend six weeks being poor in spirit and perhaps six months on mourning your sins before you can move on to meekness. If you had to do all that could be done in relation to each beatitude before you could move on to the next, there would be little hope of progress.

Maclaren is helpful here in making an observation to which we will return later. Having pointed out the order in the Beatitudes, he says,

> Now, of course, it is a mistake to expect uniformity in the process of building up character, and stages which are inseparable and successive in thought may be simultaneous and coalesce in fact. But none the less is our Lord here outlining successive stages in the growth of a true Christian life.[7]

A PRACTICAL MODEL FOR SPIRITUAL GROWTH

So here we have a practical model for growth in the Christian life. It is a biblical and practical grid for discipleship and for counseling, and it is profoundly helpful for bringing hope to friends who are battling with deeply rooted sins and addictions. Roots produce shoots and shoots bear fruit. The fruit is beautiful—forgiveness, purity, and peace—but the question, always, is how to get there.

You want to forgive, but it seems that forgiving is beyond you. You know you are supposed to forgive and you admire others who do, but you just can't get there. You've been hurt and the wounds run deep.

You struggle with impurity. Images you wish you had not seen now press into your mind, pouring fuel on the flames of your desires. You feel trapped, and you long to be free, but you don't know how to get out of this prison.

You have goals for your life and a relentless drive to pursue them. You have a vision for what you want your family, business, or church to become. But then your son or daughter rebels, your church divides, your employer no longer seems to value your contribution. You find yourself in turmoil as conflicting passions clash in the arena of your soul, and as this churning increases within you, it spills out onto the people around you. You long to have peace, but you don't know where to begin.

When you want to forgive but feel that you can't, long for purity but feel that it is beyond you, or look for peace and wonder where you can find it, the question you are really asking is how you get to the blessing promised in the fifth, sixth, or seventh beatitudes. And there can only be one answer: you get to the blessings of the last three beatitudes by means of the first four. Nourish the roots and you get shoots; water the shoots and you will get the fruits.

MOVING FROM RING TO RING

Now let's change the analogy and use an image that gave rise to the title of this book. Picture a series of seven rings, each suspended on a rope from a high ceiling. At either end of these rings there is a high platform, and your goal is to get from one platform to the other by swinging from ring to ring. You climb the platform and the first ring is within your reach. If you pull it back and swing on it, your *momentum* will bring you within reach of the second ring, and swinging on the second will bring you within reach of the third.

I've found it helpful to think of the Beatitudes as being like this series of rings. Purity of heart is the sixth ring, and there's only one way to get there. You have to climb the platform and swing through the first five.

Try to settle this simple image in your mind. To move from one ring to the next, you must grasp each ring in order. The only way to get to the fifth ring of forgiveness, the sixth ring of purity, or the seventh ring of peace is by means of the rings that come before. You can't start from the fifth, sixth, or seventh ring. They have to be *reached*, and the Beatitudes will show you how.

The good news is that the first ring is within your reach. "Blessed are the poor in spirit" (Matt. 5:3). That means, as we will see, that blessing begins when you realize that you don't have what it takes. In the kindness of God, the need that you feel for forgiveness, purity, and peace in your life is what gets you onto the first ring.

If you are a believer in Christ, but you feel stuck in your Christian life, this book is for you. If you are battling with a compulsive sin or addiction and long to have greater strength in your struggle against temptation, this book is for you. If you have the privilege of mentoring, counseling, or discipling other believers, this book is for you. If you have a great desire for holiness but feel that the progress you have made is much less than the distance you still have to travel, this book is for you.

Welcome to the gymnasium. The rings are suspended above you. Climb the platform with me, take a firm hold on the first ring, and get ready to swing.

"Blessed are the poor in spirit, for theirs is the kingdom of heaven."

MATTHEW 5:3

1

I BRING NOTHING

THE ENIGMA OF EMPTY-HANDEDNESS

Some months ago, Karen and I decided to visit the Art Institute in Chicago. It is a vast place, much bigger than we had expected, and when we saw how large it was, I said to Karen, "We need a plan."

We had about four hours and so, having found a map, we worked out a route that would make it possible for us to see the whole place in the time available, assuming that we didn't stop for too long in any of the rooms.

When we had agreed on the plan, I said, "Right. Now let's see the Art Institute!" And we did. It was a marvelous day and, having completed our tour, I felt pretty good about what we had done.

A few weeks later, a friend from England, who is an artist, came to stay in our home. In the course of conversation, she asked us about Chicago's Art Institute.

"Oh yes," I said, "we've been there."

"What did you see?" she asked.

"We saw everything," I said.

It was obvious that she was not impressed.

"Oh no," she said, "that's not the way to do it. When I go to an art gallery, I go to see three or four things, and I spend time with them." I felt rather foolish. In our race to see everything, there was a profound sense in which we had seen nothing.

The artist's counsel is helpful when it comes to the Bible. You've been reading the Bible. That's great. But what have you seen? It is possible to race through the halls of Scripture, moving past the life-transforming truths that are all around you, and yet to remain largely unaffected. But wisdom takes a different approach. She stops beside a masterpiece and looks at it until its beauty passes through her eyes and into her soul.

As the Beatitudes have worked their way into my life, it has become clear to me that this is a place where we need to linger, until these words of Jesus press themselves inside us and impart some of the great blessing that they hold.

Our Lord tells us that the poor in spirit are blessed. What does this mean? *Poor* means that you don't have much, and there's nothing particularly blessed about that. If being poor could bring us into the blessing of God, your path of progress would be simple: renounce wealth and embrace poverty. But here's the problem: wealth and poverty each bring their own temptations, and for this reason, Scripture gives us this prayer:

> *Give me neither poverty nor riches;*
> *feed me with the food that is needful for me,*
> *lest I be full and deny you and say, "Who is the Lord?"*
> *or lest I be poor and steal*
> *and profane the name of my God.*
> —Proverbs 30:8–9

30

Money is a gift and a trust from God, but getting more of it will not bring you under God's blessing any more than having less of it can keep you outside.

Luke's gospel includes a shortened account of the Beatitudes in which we find four of the eight blessings recorded in Matthew, along with four warnings or "woes." In this shortened account, our Lord says, "Blessed are you who are poor, for yours is the kingdom of God" (Luke 6:20). But we should understand the shortened form in the light of the fuller statement of Jesus, where He specifically defines the poverty that is blessed as being "poor *in spirit*."

What would being poor in spirit look like in real life? Suppose that the most gifted football player on a high school team is a follower of Jesus. Does this mean that when he turns up for practice he should say to the coach, "Hey, Coach, my game's no good. I don't think I'm worth my place on the team. Maybe you should pick somebody else"?

When a Christian goes for a job interview, and the interviewer asks, "Now tell me, why we should give you this job?", should a Christian respond by saying, "Well, I'm not sure that you should. There are others who could do this job better than me"?

No. Being poor in spirit has nothing to do with false modesty that denies your God-given gifts and talents. "Poor in spirit" means that you recognize your poverty *before God*. It is an attitude toward yourself in which you know and affirm that you have not lived the life to which God has called you, and that, without Him, you cannot do so now.

To be poor in spirit is the first mark of a person who walks with God. You may be a multitalented sports star or a high flyer in business. You may be a mega mother, a brilliant musician, a technical guru, or a political genius, but if you have truly met with God, you will know that you do not have what He requires of you.

A GREAT PROPHET LOST BEFORE GOD

Isaiah was a gifted and godly preacher, and the people of his day would have celebrated this silver-tongued prophet for his remarkable ministry. If he were in ministry today, people would be cramming into conferences to hear him speak, and if he were on Twitter, he would have millions of followers.

Sometime into his ministry, Isaiah had a remarkable experience in which he saw a vision of God "sitting upon a throne, high and lifted up" (Isa. 6:1). The sheer size of the throne dwarfed everything else. Giving us a sense of scale, Isaiah says that the train of God's robe filled the temple. God is greater by far than all that was going on in the temple. His presence makes everything else look small.

Angelic creatures flew above and around the throne, calling out to each other, "Holy, holy, holy is the Lord of hosts; the whole earth is full of his glory." When this announcement was made, the foundations of the building shook, smoke filled the temple, and Isaiah, the gifted and godly prophet said, "Woe is me! For I am lost" (vv. 1–5).

If Isaiah pronounces himself lost in the presence of God, where would that leave the rest of us? The world saw Isaiah's gifts and talents, but in the presence of God, Isaiah saw only his own need. Coming into proximity with God made him poor in spirit.

Pride can only live in the soul of a person who is far from God. It puts its foot on the gas to get you as far from God as possible because pride cannot exist in the presence of God. When God comes near, pride has to go. So picture this: the smoke of God's presence coming down into the temple of your life, and pride staggering out from your soul, coughing and spluttering because it cannot live in the awesome presence of God. This is what happened to Isaiah. In the presence of God, the gifted prophet became poor in spirit.

The gifted football player has much to offer his team. He will be celebrated at school. He will be offered scholarships and all the rest of it. But if he has any knowledge of God at all, he knows, with Isaiah, that he is among the poorest of the poor.

The gifted graduate has a talent that she can offer to her company. She graduates summa cum laude, and she will be fast-tracked for promotion. She will draw the company of other gifted people who want to attach themselves to her because she's going somewhere. But if she knows God at all, she sees that however much attention she receives, and however celebrated she may become, she stands before God empty-handed.

BEING HUMBLE IN A SELF-AFFIRMING CULTURE

Becoming poor in spirit goes against the grain of our self-affirming culture. Writing in Great Britain in the 1950s, Martyn Lloyd-Jones described the mood of his time: "Express yourself, believe in yourself, realize the powers that are innate in yourself and let the whole world see and know them." That is the spirit of the age.[1]

Not much has changed today! In our culture of affirmation, it sometimes seems that parents, teachers, counselors, politicians, and advertisers all conspire to tell us how great we are, and apart from a miracle of God's grace, we will believe them.

Wisdom calls us to trust God and doubt ourselves. "Trust in the Lord with all your heart, and do not lean on your own understanding" (Prov. 3:5). But our culture turns that on its head and says, "Trust yourself and doubt God." That inversion is as old as the garden of Eden, and it's all around us.

The teaching of Jesus is directly opposed to the creed that says, "Believe in yourself." Jesus does not say, "Believe in yourself." He says, "Believe in God; believe also in me" (John 14:1). The person who says, "Believe in yourself," is putting himself or herself in the place of God.

The person who is far from God will often feel that she has the ability to face whatever challenge comes her way. "I can do this! I'm up for it! I can handle it!" But the person who walks with God will say something different: "Because he is at my right hand, I shall not be shaken" (Ps. 16:8). There is all the difference in the world between these two things.

I'm a dad, and having raised two sons, I've stood on the sidelines at their games and shouted "You can do it!" with everyone else. I regularly tell my sons that I am proud of them. Affirmation matters. But let's be thoughtful about how we speak to our children, especially in the teachable moments of life. It is not a good reflection of faith in Jesus Christ for a father, mother, counselor, or friend to pump a Christian's ego by constantly reinforcing the "You can do it" message that pervades our culture. It is a far better reflection of faith to say something like, "The Lord is with you and He will not fail you, and in Christ you can do all things."

Do you see the difference between these two ways of speaking? One is godless. It puts self in the place of God and exalts the individual to the place of the divine. The other reflects the humility of one who knows that his or her strength lies in the presence and the blessing of a sovereign God.

Pursuing humility will be a challenge, not only because it goes against the grain of our culture, but also because it goes against the trajectory of all religion. Religion works on the idea that you must live a life that is pleasing to God in order to win His favor. Every religion in the world offers some variation on this theme. Did you make the right choices? Pursue the right disciplines? Follow the right paths? At the end of the day, this approach boils down to merit. Did you earn it? And that trajectory always promotes pride.

If you read the Bible, pray, serve in the church, and try to pursue a good and moral life, your flesh will announce to you that you have done something good. Then it will occur to you that others should do the same and before you know it, arrogance will have crept in through the back door of your attempts at a godly life.

A third challenge in pursuing humility is that the blessing of God makes humility harder. Here's the irony: the poor in spirit experience the blessing of God, but the more you experience this blessing, the harder it is to remain poor in spirit.

The more successful you are, the easier it is to believe that you are something, and the harder it is to humble yourself before God. If your children believe while others are rebelling; if your marriage prospers while your friend's is falling apart; if your business succeeds while others fail; if your ministry grows when others are in decline, it is hard to avoid the sneaking feeling that you must have done something right. Success of any sort, in any sphere, tends to make us think that we are something special.

So if you are religious, reasonably successful, and live in a self-affirming culture, the pursuit of humility will be a steep climb for you. Thank God for the work of the Holy Spirit, who comes to convince us of sin, righteousness, and judgment (John 16:9). Without Him we would never know the blessing that belongs to the poor in spirit.

What do you know of this poverty of spirit in your own life?

People who are poor in spirit don't flaunt their gifts. They don't blame their sins and failings on others. Instead, they are unimpressed with their own attempts at living a godly life. As Thomas Watson says, "The poor in spirit, when he acts most like a saint, confesses himself 'the chief of sinners.' He blushes more at the defects of his graces than others do at the excess of their sins."[2]

In a world where personalities loom big and God is often regarded as a prop on the stage of our own performance, people who are poor in spirit know that they are a small blip on the radar screen of eternity. They know that God is glorious and awesome in His holiness. They know that He owes them nothing and they see that, even if viewed at their best, they are unworthy servants who hang and depend completely on the mercy of God.

ENJOYING A TASTE OF HEAVEN

To be poor in spirit is where the blessing of God begins. This is the gateway blessing that leads to all the others, and without this none of the other blessings can be reached.

The blessing promised to the poor in spirit is "the kingdom of heaven," and it is promised in the present tense. "Blessed are the poor in spirit, for theirs *is* the kingdom of heaven" (Matt. 5:3, emphasis added).

Since heaven is a future blessing, we might have expected Jesus to say, "Blessed are the poor in spirit, because theirs *will be* the kingdom of heaven." But our Lord doesn't say that.

What makes this present-tense promise even more striking is that all of the other blessings are promised for the future:

"Blessed are those who mourn, for they *shall be* comforted" (v. 4).

"Blessed are the meek, for they *shall* inherit the earth" (v. 5).

"Blessed are those who hunger and thirst for righteousness, for they *shall be* satisfied" (v. 6, all emphases added).

But the promise of heaven breaks the pattern. "Blessed are the poor in spirit, for theirs *is* the kingdom of heaven." That's present tense—Jesus is talking about a taste of heaven that you can enjoy now.

Life in this world is a long way from heaven, and the things that may come to your mind when you think of heaven are a world away from the realities of earth. Streets of gold? I've never seen one. Redeemed people made perfect? Not where I live. Lions lying down with lambs? Nations no longer waging war? Every tear wiped from our eyes? None of this is ours yet. So what taste of heaven can the poor in spirit have *now*?

The poor in spirit taste the greatest blessing of heaven, which is the presence of God. As the Almighty declared to Isaiah: "Thus says the One who is high and lifted up, who inhabits eternity, whose name is

Holy: I dwell in the high and holy place, and also with him who is of a contrite and lowly spirit" (57:15).

Do you see what is being said here? The sovereign Lord of the universe lives in two places. He dwells in heaven, the high and holy place, but He also lives with the person who has a contrite and lowly spirit. Heaven is to live with God, and the poor in spirit get a taste of it, because God comes to live with them. Heaven comes to the humble before the humble get to heaven.

This same truth is repeated in the Psalms: "The Lord is near to the brokenhearted and saves the crushed in spirit" (34:18). And again, "For though the Lord is high, he regards the lowly, but the haughty he knows from afar" (138:6).

God knows the proud from afar, but He lives with the lowly. If you want to move beyond relating to God from a distance, and feel His presence in your life, you must begin by humbling yourself.

This promise of God's presence with the poor in spirit opens the door of hope, because the blessing is promised not on the basis of what we have, but of what we lack. C. H. Spurgeon describes the paradox of this first beatitude:

> It is worthy of double mention that this first blessing is given rather to the absence than to the presence of praiseworthy qualities; it is a blessing, not upon the man who is distinguished for this virtue or remarkable for that excellence, but upon him whose chief characteristic is that he confesses his own sad deficiencies. . . . Not what I have, but what I have not, is the first point of contact between my soul and God.[3]

God can use brutal circumstances in your life to bring you to a place of being poor in spirit. When you find yourself saying, "I don't have what it takes to face this," God says to you, "I will dwell with you here."

When you feel overwhelmed by the power of temptation, God can use the intensity of your struggle to shatter your pride and make you poor in spirit. And if that should happen, the battle that brought you to the brink of despair can be the means of bringing you to a new place of blessing.

There is hope for you here when you know that you have messed up. If your failure should lead you to genuine humility before God, Christ will come and live with you, and the very sin that would have led you down the road to hell may, in God's kindness, be the means by which you find the path that leads to heaven.

People who feel they have something to offer God come to Him with their hands full, but as long as our hands are full, we are not in a position to receive. Watson says, "If the hand is full of pebbles, it cannot receive gold."[4]

People who are poor in spirit drop the pebbles because they want the gold and they know that it can only be received by empty-handed believers. When you know that you have nothing to offer God, you are in a position to receive all that He offers to you. When you accept that you cannot claim His blessing as a right, you are in a position to receive it as a gift. Empty-handedness is where the blessing of God begins.

SEVEN BLESSINGS FOR EMPTY-HANDED BELIEVERS

1. Empty-handedness will release you from the idea that God owes you.

God is your Creator. That means that He owns you and that you have a duty toward Him. But it is easy, especially in our culture, to forget this and slide into thinking that God is the one who has a duty toward us. We get the idea that we are the ones who should be writing a job description for God, a kind of Ten Commandments for what we require of Him: "Thou shalt provide a level of income that will sustain our chosen lifestyle. Thou shalt give us joy and fulfillment in mutually satisfying relationships. Thou shalt insulate our loved ones from the sufferings experienced by others in this world." And woe to God if He does not meet our expectations!

Do you see how pride is written all over this kind of thinking? Pride says, "I gave something to God, and now He owes me something bigger and better back." As long as your heart is there, you are on a path to bitterness, disappointment, and resentment.

The blessing of God belongs not to those who list their demands, but to the poor in spirit who humble themselves before Him.

The person who is poor in spirit says: "I owe God *everything*, and I can give Him *nothing*. God owes me *nothing*, and He has given me *everything*." When you are poor in spirit, you will be delivered from the lie that God owes you better than you had in your past and better than you have right now.

2. Empty-handedness will position you to ask and receive in prayer.

Thomas Watson says, "A poor man is ever begging," and "He who is poor in spirit is much in prayer."[5] People who know their own need have an active prayer life, and when they pray they ask!

Jesus told a story about a Pharisee and a tax collector (Luke 18:9–14). Both of them pray, but their prayers are very different. The Pharisee prays about himself, "God, I thank you that I am not like other men, extortioners, unjust, adulterers" (Luke 18:11). The striking thing about this man's prayer is that he does not ask for anything. He asks for nothing and he receives nothing. Why does this man not ask? Because in his heart, he thinks that he already has what it takes. He is not poor in spirit.

But the tax collector, with his head hanging in shame, asks, "God, be merciful to me, a sinner!" (Luke 18:13). The tax collector asks of God because he knows his own need. He is poor in spirit, and Jesus says that this man, not the other, went home blessed, justified, and forgiven.

3. Empty-handedness will help you to bear affliction.

The apostle Peter wrote to Christians in a culture that, like ours, was fast becoming antagonistic toward believers. "Do not be surprised," he said, "at the fiery trial when it comes upon you to test you, as though something strange were happening to you" (1 Peter 4:12).

How do you prepare, as a Christian, when you know that trials lie ahead? You humble yourself under the mighty hand of God, because

GAINING MOMENTUM / Seven Blessings for the Empty-Handed

1. *Empty-handedness releases you from the idea that God owes you.* The person who is poor in spirit says: "I owe God everything, and I can give Him nothing. God owes me nothing, and He has given me everything." When we list demands, we are moving toward bitterness, disappointment, and resentment. The blessing of God belongs to those who humble themselves before Him.

2. *Empty-handedness positions you to ask and receive in prayer.* When we come to God in humility to ask His help, we are recognizing we are needy. Jesus says that the person who comes to Him recognizing his or her need for divine help will be blessed and forgiven, just as the tax collector was (cf. Luke 18:13–14).

3. *Empty-handedness helps you to bear affliction.* God opposes proud people, but to the humble He gives grace to endure. That truth may not seem logical if you read stories of proud conquerors or are told, "When times get tough, the tough keep going." Yet Scripture says "God opposes the proud but gives grace to the humble" (1 Peter 5:5). So it follows that humility will help you to endure every affliction, whether poverty, poor health, or some other trial.

God opposes the proud but gives grace to the humble (1 Peter 5:5–6).

If I give way to pride, God will stand against me, and I will come under His discipline. "Everyone who is arrogant in heart is an abomination to the Lord" (Prov. 16:5). An abomination! So God stands in the way of the proud. He opposes them. But to the humble He gives grace. The pursuit of humility might not be the first strategy you would think of for finding strength to face difficulty, but since God gives grace to the humble, it follows that humility will help you to endure in times of trial.

4. *Empty-handedness nourishes your love for others.* Pride is like a bucket of water poured out on the fires of love in any relationship. Seeking to exalt yourself or place someone in an inferior relationship has damaged many family relationships, whether a wife to her husband or a father to his son. But humility can fan the dying embers of love into a flame. Love gets choked by the weeds of pride, but it grows and thrives in the soil of a humble heart.

5. *Empty-handedness strengthens you to overcome temptation.* If pride leads to falling, as the Bible says (Prov. 16:8; 1 Cor. 10:12), it follows that humility helps you to stand. By pursuing humility, you will strike a blow at the master sin of pride, and in this way you will subdue the temptation of many other sins.

6. *Empty-handedness releases you from the tyranny of self.* The victorious Christian neither exalts nor downgrades himself. His interests have shifted from self to Christ. What he is or is not no longer concerns him. He believes that he has been crucified with Christ. With this focus on Christ, we will neither elevate nor deprecate ourselves.

7. *Empty-handedness leads you to worship Jesus.* The more you see in yourself, the less you will see in Christ, and the more you see in Christ, the less you will see in yourself. Once you and I see the poverty of our own position before God, we can recognize the glorious gift of Jesus Christ. And seeing that all your good has its source in Him will lead you to worship the Savior.

4. Empty-handedness will nourish your love for others.

Pride is always self-seeking and it is easily provoked. It is the opposite of love, which does not boast and "is not irritable or resentful" (1 Cor. 13:5). Pride will be like a bucket of water poured out on the fires of love in any marriage. But humility can fan the dying embers of love into a flame.

If you are in a relationship that has come under strain or perhaps has been broken in a way that makes you wonder if love could ever be restored, think about this: the greatest story of reconciliation in a broken relationship is the story of God reconciling with us through Jesus Christ. How did Christ go about this? The first move of the Savior was that He humbled Himself (Phil. 2:8). He took the form of a servant. That is how the great reconciliation began, and Christ says that your attitude should be the same as His (Phil. 2:5). Love gets choked by the weeds of pride, but it grows and thrives in the soil of a humble heart.

5. Empty-handedness will strengthen you to overcome temptation.

We noted earlier that being poor in spirit is a gateway blessing, an entry point that leads to other blessings. In the same way, pride is a gateway sin that opens the door to many other sins. We read in the book of Proverbs that "pride goes before destruction, and a haughty spirit before a fall" (16:18). The New Testament version of this truth is, "Let anyone who thinks that he stands take heed lest he fall" (1 Cor. 10:12).

Now, if pride leads to falling, it follows that humility will help you to stand. When you know that your flesh is weak, you will watch and pray so that you do not fall into temptation (Matt. 26:41). By pursuing humility you will strike a blow at the master sin of pride, and in this way you will subdue the power of many other sins and open the door to many other blessings.

6. Empty-handedness will release you from the tyranny of self.

Self has more than one way of making you a slave, and if the focus on pride in this chapter seems remote to you, it could be that, rather than being trapped by self-love, you have been ambushed through self-loathing.

Self-loathing is a painful struggle for some people. If this is your battle, you will know what it is to wake up feeling that you hate yourself, and at some point you may even have thought about harming yourself. Self-loathing may seem a long way from self-love, but both are expressions of the same preoccupation with self.

"Self, whether swaggering or groveling, can never be anything but hateful to God," A. W. Tozer wrote. "Boasting is an evidence that we are pleased with self; belittling, that we are disappointed in it."[6]

Tozer's point is simple: boasting and belittling are equally focused on self. In the end, it really doesn't make much difference whether you destroy yourself by your swaggering or by your groveling. Self may exalt you or self may condemn you but either way, self is in control, and self is always a tyrant. But if you cultivate humility, the tyrant will be overthrown.

As Tozer points out,

> The victorious Christian neither exalts nor downgrades himself. His interests have shifted from self to Christ. What he is or is not no longer concerns him. He believes that he has been crucified with Christ and he is not willing either to praise or deprecate such a man.[7]

7. Empty-handedness will lead you to worship Jesus.

The more you see in yourself, the less you will see in Christ, and the more you see in Christ, the less you will see in yourself. Spurgeon says, "Christ is never precious till we are poor in spirit. We must see our own wants before we can perceive his wealth; pride blinds the eyes, and sincere humility must open them, or the beauties of Jesus will be forever hidden from us."[8]

When you see the poverty of your own position before God, the gift of Jesus Christ will seem overwhelmingly glorious to you, and seeing all your good in Him will lead you to worship.

Here is the difference between a hypocrite and a true child of God: people who are far from God make much of themselves, and people who live near to God make much of Jesus Christ. People who are far from God focus on what they are doing for Him; people who live near to God find joy in what He is doing for them. They join with Paul in saying, "Far be it from me to boast except in the cross of our Lord Jesus Christ" (Gal. 6:14).

HOW TO CULTIVATE HUMILITY

When you remodel a house, there are invariably two stages in the process: demolition and renovation. You begin with the "demo" day. Old carpet gets torn up; old cabinets and counters are ripped out. If you are a do-it-yourselfer, you even get to swing the sledgehammer at the wall!

The pursuit of humility begins with doing a "demo" on pride. In Alexander Maclaren's memorable words, we must "rip up this swollen bladder of self-esteem."[9]

How to Begin the Demo

A good place to begin the demolition is by regularly examining yourself in the light of God's Word. Measure yourself by what God calls you to pursue. So, for example, when you read in 1 Corinthians 13 that "love does not insist on its own way," ask yourself, "Where am I insisting on my own way?" When you read that "love is not irritable or resentful," ask God to bring to your mind where you may have fallen into these sins.

Growing up in Scotland, I learned some simple questions that I still use when reading the Bible. Is there a promise to believe? A command to obey? A sin to avoid? A warning to heed? An example to follow? Each of these questions will help you to demolish pride. Am I believing this promise? Am I obeying this command? Have I fallen into this sin? Am I hearing this warning? Am I following this example?

Use the Word of God as a mirror, and make sure that you take a good look at yourself in this mirror every day. Ask God to show you yourself when you read the Bible, and then measure yourself by what you read. The law reveals our sinfulness. Keep the mirror—God's Word—before you and you will soon find yourself saying, as every true Christian does, "Lord, I fall a long way short of what You are calling me to be and to do." You will feel your need of Christ and you will discover what it is to be poor in spirit.

From Demo to Reno

But there's more to being poor in spirit than knowing and confessing your sins. Jesus was humble, and there was no sin in Him. The humility of Jesus did not spring from an awareness of sin, because He had none. It came from another source.

Andrew Murray is the writer who opened this up for me: "If humility is to be our joy we must see that it is not only the mark of shame because of sin, but, apart from all sin, humility is being clothed upon with the very beauty and blessedness of heaven and of Jesus."[10]

Pause and linger over these words: "Humility . . . the very beauty and blessedness of Jesus." That's what we are to pursue. Far from the world of guilt and shame, humility is something beautiful. The reason you use the sledgehammer of the law to demolish pride, pretense, and self-righteousness in your life is that they must be taken out in order to make way for something beautiful. The "demo" makes way for the "reno." The old and ugly is removed so that the new and beautiful may be installed.

Murray goes on to explain that "humility is something deeper than contrition. "It is our participation in the life of Jesus."[11]

Being poor in spirit is part of becoming like Jesus, who humbled Himself. He said,

> "I can do nothing on my own" (John 5:30).
> "I have come down from heaven not to do my own will" (John 6:38).
> "I do not seek my own glory" (John 8:50).

Since these are the words of the Son of God, how much more should they be mine? The blessedness of Jesus is seen in His gentle and lowly heart. In pursuing humility, you are reflecting the beauty of His life.

So examine yourself in the light of the Word of God and model yourself on the Son of God, knowing that God lives with the humble, and that the people who know their poverty before God are the ones who are blessed. As Watson puts it, "How poor are they that think themselves rich! How rich are they that see themselves poor!"[12]

The main theme of this book is that the Beatitudes map out a path for progress in the Christian life. Ahead of us are other blessings that include forgiveness, purity, and peace, but I'm glad that the Beatitudes don't start there. If being pure in heart were the starting point for growth in the Christian life, nobody would ever get there. But it's not. Being poor in spirit is! Thank God, the starting point is to recognize that we do not have what it takes.

I encourage you to grasp this first ring today. Humble yourself. Come to Jesus Christ today and tell Him that you do not have what it takes to live a holy life. Tell Him that you do not have the power to change. Ask Him to give to you what you do not have, and then trust Him, look to Him, believing His promise that He will come to you, live with you, and bless you. Christians know their own poverty. They look to Jesus for what they do not have, and find in Him all that they need.

"Blessed are those who mourn, for they shall be comforted."

MATTHEW 5:4

I TAKE OWNERSHIP

THE POWER OF SPIRITUAL MOURNING

Mourning can be a miserable business, and I wouldn't be surprised if you were tempted to skip this chapter and move on to something else that looks more promising.

But that would be a mistake. Jesus speaks of a kind of mourning that is blessed and, as we will see in this chapter, learning the art of spiritual mourning is crucial to your progress in the Christian life.

If you are like me, you may wonder how the words "mourning" and "blessed" can possibly belong in the same sentence. What is this mourning that Jesus says is blessed? There are three very different kinds of mourning, and it is important to distinguish between them.

The first of these is *natural mourning*—the grief that comes through the loss of a loved one. If God has given you the wonderful gift of a person who is dear to you, and that person has been taken away, your natural and proper response will be to mourn, and when you do, it is good to remember that Jesus has been here too. He wept at the grave of a dearly loved friend (John 11:35). The presence and comfort of Jesus in the journey through bereavement is a treasured gift from God, but it is not what our Lord is speaking about here.

In the Beatitudes, Jesus speaks about qualities that we should pro-actively pursue, conditions of heart that are so laden with blessing that we are to get as much of them in our lives as we possibly can. God calls you to go after peace and purity, to pursue meekness and mercy, and to hunger and thirst for righteousness. You can never get too much of these things.

But how could that be true of natural mourning? No one who is going through the sorrow of bereavement would say, "I want to go after as much of this grief as I can possibly get." So while it is a treasured truth that Christ walks with the believer in the valley of bereavement, this is not what our Lord is speaking about here.

There's a second and very different kind of mourning that, far from being natural, is actually sinful. This sinful mourning is a pining after something that God did not give you. Notice the contrast: Natural mourning is grief over something given by God and then taken away. But *sinful mourning* is grieving over something that God never intended you to have.

An example of this is found in the story of Ahab, one of the kings of Israel (1 Kings 21). God gave him a palace and a kingdom, despite the fact that he was a wretched king. Beyond the boundary of the palace grounds, he saw a small vineyard that belonged to a poor man. The king set his eye, and then his heart, on this little vineyard and, over time, he became increasingly obsessed with it. He offered to buy the vineyard from its owner, Naboth. But the vineyard had been given to

Naboth's family as a trust from the Lord, and this poor man was not for selling at any price.

The king became "vexed and sullen" (v. 4). He pouted around the palace because he coveted a gift that God had given to someone else and not to him. This pining after something that God never intended him to have consumed the king, and eventually it led him to murder Naboth, bringing the opposite of blessing into Ahab's life. Grieving over something that God never intended you to have is a sinful kind of mourning. It is always a killer and it is clearly not what our Lord had in mind when He spoke about the mourning that is blessed.

A PROPER, SPIRITUAL MOURNING

A third and very different kind of mourning involves sorrow over our sins against God, and it is this *spiritual mourning* that Jesus describes as blessed. Spiritual mourning is the godly sorrow that produces repentance, and it is blessed because it leads to life (2 Cor. 7:10). The more you have of this kind of mourning in your life, the more blessed you will be.

Spiritual mourning is an art that Christians desperately need to rediscover today. It is key to tackling what we sometimes call "habitual sin," that is, a sin that a person may fall into repeatedly over a long period of time. If a particular sin has become habitual for you or you would describe yourself as addicted to a certain form of behavior, you need to learn all that you can about spiritual mourning. God's purpose for your life is not that you remain stuck in a cycle of sinning, saying "sorry" to God, and then repeating the same behavior. Spiritual mourning will break that cycle by bringing you to a place where you grieve over your sin, see its cost, and make a decisive break from it.

This subject is of huge importance for the church today because we are surrounded by a form of faith that bears no resemblance to biblical Christianity. For more than a half century a true faith that unites a person to Jesus Christ has been replaced by an assent to, or agreement with, certain beliefs. This substitution makes it easy for many to "accept Christ" without ever pursuing the holiness of life to which a Christian is called. Non-Christians despise this emaciated form of faith, and they are right to do so. A form of faith that leaves a person essentially unchanged is not worthy to bear the name of our Lord.

FORSAKING SIN AND RETURNING TO GOD

A second gutting of biblical Christianity is that repentance, which in the Bible involves a change of direction, is often reduced to "admitting that I am a sinner," and asking for forgiveness.

Isaiah described true repentance when he said:

> Seek the Lord while he may be found; call upon him while he is near; let the wicked forsake his way, and the unrighteous man his thoughts; let him return to the Lord, that he may have compassion on him, and to our God, for he will abundantly pardon. (Isa. 55:6–7)

Seeking the Lord involves leaving or forsaking ways and thoughts that dishonor Him, and calling on the Lord involves returning to Him.

God says to the sinner, "You must forsake your way! Leave it! Abandon it! Be done with your wicked thoughts!" There's more here than admitting that you are a sinner. Much more! You can admit that you are a sinner and continue in the sins you admit, but God calls us to a decisive change of behavior and direction in which a person quits his sin and returns to the Lord.

The New Testament version of this truth is found in 2 Timothy 2:19, where Paul writes, "God's firm foundation stands, bearing this seal: 'The Lord knows those who are his,' and, 'Let everyone who names the name of the Lord depart from iniquity.'"

Here is something foundational to biblical Christianity: if you are a follower of Christ, you've got to depart from iniquity. Faith and repentance are two sides of the same coin, and they belong inseparably together. God's people repent as they believe and they believe as they repent. Faith is the bond of a living union with Jesus and, for this reason, it is also the wellspring of repentance toward Him.

But if a generation grows up believing that Christianity boils down to agreeing with certain beliefs, admitting that you are a sinner, and asking to be forgiven, it will not be surprising to find many who count themselves Christian and are confident of going to heaven without ever pursuing the repentance that is central to the calling of God for all of His people.

We are surrounded by a form of faith that has been reshaped to accommodate our continuing indulgence, and the result is a growing number of people who admit that they are sinners and "accept Jesus" without ever having experienced new life in Jesus Christ.

They don't feel poor in spirit, they don't know what it is to mourn over their own sins, and they don't submit themselves meekly to God. Without these roots, they do not have a deep hunger and thirst for righteousness, and knowing little about mercy, purity, and peace, they live at a distance from the blessing of God.

Replacing faith with accepting certain truths and exchanging repentance for admitting that we are sinners has been a disaster for true Christianity in our time. We desperately need to rediscover the joy of biblical repentance and the blessing of spiritual mourning.

SIX ELEMENTS OF SPIRITUAL MOURNING

Having seen why spiritual mourning matters, we now need to define more closely what spiritual mourning is and show how you can make progress in your Christian life by swinging on this second ring.

Spiritual mourning is a heartfelt sorrow over particular sins, arising from humility and infused with hope, that leads you to forsake these sins at the cross.

There are six elements in this definition, each pointing to an aspect of the character, focus, motive, or outcome of spiritual mourning. Together, they describe the process by which you can break the cycle of repeating the same sins and go for growth in your Christian life.

1. Spiritual mourning names particular sins.

Spiritual mourning is a heartfelt sorrow over *particular sins,* arising from humility and infused with hope, that leads you to forsake these sins at the cross.

Spiritual mourning always has a clear focus. It is mourning over named sins, and this is very different from grieving over a general sense of unworthiness or of failure. Satan loves to depress Christians with a general sense of our own inadequacy, but nothing good can come from this. How can you address a general sense of failure, unworthiness, or inadequacy? You cannot. It is a dead end. Mourning over sin in general never moves you forward. It just leaves you feeling miserable, and sometimes it can be a convenient way to avoid facing up to the real sins of your life.

Spiritual mourning relates to specific sins, and the first step in cultivating this mourning is to name one or more sins, stating them clearly without excuse and without evasion. "I have acted out of envy. I have insisted on my own way. I have deceived and I have covered up, and this is a sin against God."

Spurgeon is clear and helpful in his pastoral counsel here:

> The first advice I give you is this: Particularize your sins. Do not say, "I am a sinner." It means nothing. Everybody says that. But say this, "Am I a liar? Am I a thief? Am I a drunkard? Have I had unchaste thoughts? Have I committed unclean acts? Have I in my soul often rebelled against God? Am I often angry without a cause? Have I a bad temper? Am I covetous? Do I love this world better than the world to come? Do I neglect prayer?

... Put the questions upon the separate points, and you will soon convict yourself much more readily than by taking yourself in the gross [in general] as being a sinner.[1]

Notice the focus in all these questions. Spurgeon is encouraging you to look for specific sins that lurk in the dark corners of your soul. Imagine walking through a dark basement. Hidden treasures are stored there, perhaps unopened gifts as well. But there's also a lot of junk and trash; and there's a bad smell because of some animals that slipped into the basement through a broken window and died there. Hidden in the corners, some living animals may be lurking as well. That rather unattractive scene is a biblical picture of your soul.

God could show you the full horror of the state of your soul by turning on the basement floodlight at any time, but if He did that, you would be overwhelmed, and you would not know where to begin in cleaning up the mess. No Christian could bear to know the full extent of his or her sin if all were revealed at the same time. But God is patient and in His kindness He will show you the ugly truth about your own heart not with a floodlight but with a flashlight. He will lead you through the murky basement, gradually and progressively illuminating what hides in the dark corners of your soul, so that by God's grace you can deal with the junk as He shows it to you.

Spiritual mourning begins with seeing your sins, but by nature we don't see well. Our instinct is to justify whatever we do. We don't see ourselves as others see us, let alone as God sees us. So we need the flashlight to shine into the dark corners of our souls, and God shines that light through His Word, His Spirit, and His people.

Spiritual mourning starts with an open Bible. The entrance of God's Word gives light (Ps. 119:130), and when the Scriptures have a regular entrance into your life, you will begin to see what is going on in the dark and hidden places of your heart. God will use what you read in the Bible to open your eyes to issues in your life that you may not have known to be sin, and to sins in your life that you did not know were present.

The questions we reviewed in the last chapter will help you here: as you hear a passage from the Bible read in church and as you read it on your own during the week, ask yourself, "Is there a sin here for me to avoid?"

Practice using the Bible to identify hidden sins that might be lurking in your life. If, in the passage you are reading, there is not an obvious sin to avoid, use the other questions. If there is a promise, ask whether you believe it or could you be missing what God offers because of unbelief. If there is an example, ask yourself to what extent you are following the example, or if you on a different path. If there is a command, ask yourself if you are obeying the command, and if there is a warning, ask yourself if you are heeding this warning or are in danger of following a destructive path.

Get used to identifying particular sins when you read the Bible. You will begin to see what God sees and you will get to know what grieves and offends Him.

When you have identified a particular sin, you can ask the Lord to show you where that sin may be lurking in your life. So for example, when you read from 1 Corinthians 13, "Love is patient and kind; love does not envy or boast; it is not arrogant or rude" (vv. 4–5), you are immediately confronted with six specific sins: impatience, unkindness, envy, boasting, pride, and rudeness. So where have I been rude? Who might I have envied? Where am I being impatient? Framing these questions will be like turning on the flashlight in the basement of your soul. The Bible will show you what sins to look for and the Holy Spirit will show you where they are found. Ask Him to search your heart and to open your eyes to hidden sins, even as David did (Ps. 139:23–24).

Other Christians can also help you in this area. Honest relationships with other believers who know you and love you are a special gift from God, not least because they give a safe place to fulfill the command of James: "Confess your sins to one another and pray for one another, that you may be healed" (James 5:16).

Here's a challenge: if you are married, ask your spouse to help you identify one sin against which you should be fighting more strongly. The person God has placed next to you is in a great position to help you, so why not ask them for that help?

Having been blessed with a happy marriage and a wonderfully perceptive wife, I have benefited greatly from this kind of honest conversation on many occasions. One of them was on a drive to Iowa where I was scheduled to speak at a conference. I can still picture where we were on the road when I said, "I've been thinking about where I need to grow and I want you to tell me one sin that you think I should be fighting against more strongly."

Karen paused and thought for a bit, and then she said, "Can I give you two?" We both laughed and then she identified, with great insight, two areas in which I needed to grow. It was profoundly helpful, and these kinds of conversations have continued to be useful to both of us as we have tried to help each other.

If you are not married or if your marriage is not at a place where there is a high level of trust, ask someone else who knows you well. Find someone who can speak honestly into your life, and listen to what they have to say.

What would help you grow as a Christian? What hinders you from being more useful to God than you are at this time? These are tough questions and you will need all the light and help you can get to answer them. God will give you that light through His Word, applied by the Spirit, and through trusted Christian friends who know you and love you well enough to speak the truth into your life, so use the means that God has given.

Spiritual mourning begins when you are able to name one or more specific sins that have lurked in your life. When you are clear that what you have named is a sin and that it really is in you, you are ready to enter into spiritual mourning.

2. Spiritual mourning involves heartfelt sorrow.

Spiritual mourning is *a heartfelt sorrow* over particular sins, arising from humility and infused with hope, that leads you to forsake these sins at the cross.

Spiritual mourning is a heartfelt sorrow. Here we focus on the important difference between admitting to a sin and being truly repentant from the heart.

After a major victory in battle, King Saul disobeyed a direct command from God by taking plunder for himself and for his men. The king cheated, deceived, and stole, and then he lied to cover it up. But Saul was found out and when his sin was exposed, he confessed: "I have sinned, for I have transgressed the commandment of the Lord" (1 Sam. 15:18–19, 24).

At first sight it would appear that Saul was genuinely repentant, but then he said something to Samuel that gave his game away. "I have sinned; yet honor me now before the elders of my people and before Israel, and return with me, that I may bow before the Lord your God" (v. 30).

Saul admitted that he had sinned, but his attention was focused on damage control. His first concern was his reputation, and that is why he wanted Samuel to honor him before the people.

Saul's life story shows the sorry path of a person who admits that he or she is wrong but does not have the heartfelt sorrow that is a signature mark of spiritual mourning. For Saul, one sin led to another, and in the end he died far from God. Saul's confession of sin was a manifestation of the worldly sorrow that Paul says produces death, and it is very different from the godly sorrow that produces repentance and leads to salvation (2 Cor. 7:10).

So how can you cultivate this heartfelt and godly sorrow? How can you practice spiritual mourning? How can you break the cycle of repeating the same sins and move forward in your Christian life?

Heartfelt sorrow over a particular sin grows when you see what it costs. Take a long, hard look at the cost of this sin to you, to others, and to Christ, and you will enter more deeply into spiritual mourning.

Begin with the cost to yourself. Think about the holy life to which God has called you. Think of where you might have been by now if this sin had not held you back. Consider how this sin has limited your usefulness to Christ. Reflect on how it has dampened your worship, dulled your testimony, and kept you at a distance from God.

Then think about other sins into which the sin you are mourning has led you: sins of deception and pretense. Look at what this sin is costing you, total up the bill, and then think of what your life could be if you left this sin behind.

Then you need to consider what this sin of yours has cost others. Nobody sins to himself or herself alone. The sin you are mourning has made you harder to live with, more difficult to work with, and tougher to love. But what if your sin is secret and others who love you know nothing about it? Even if they never find out, your sin is still costly to them because your sin diminishes you, and that robs others of what they might have received from you. Think about the husband, wife, father, mother, son, daughter, friend, colleague, employer, or employee you might have been if it were not for this sin that you are mourning. There's so much more that you might have brought to the lives of others and, as you set your heart on forsaking this sin, there is more that you can bring to others in the future.

Then think about how costly the sin you are mourning was for Jesus.

God always acts in justice. This means that there is a measured consequence for each offense. Every sin is brought to the bar of God's justice and receives the punishment that is due.

Jesus did not hang on the cross for sin in general, but for sins in particular—sins with names, dates, and faces on them. That means that Jesus suffered for the sin you are mourning. The punishment for this sin belonged to you. Every time you fell into this sin again, it accumulated, and God, in His amazing mercy, transferred the whole guilt and penalty that was due to you on account of this sin onto Jesus. Think about this: the sin that you are mourning had its place in all that Christ endured in the darkness at Calvary. He took it on Himself, and He suffered because of it.

GAINING MOMENTUM / Six Elements of Spiritual Mourning

1. *Spiritual mourning names particular sins.* True spiritual mourning begins by naming one or more sins, stating them clearly without excuse and without evasion. Declare them immediately and admit they are an offense against God. Get used to identifying particular sins when you read the Bible. You will begin to see what God sees and you will get to know what grieves and offends Him. Once you have named the sin as being really in you, you are ready to enter into spiritual mourning.

2. *Spiritual mourning involves heartfelt sorrow.* Take a long, hard look at the cost of this sin and you will enter more deeply into spiritual mourning. First think about other sins into which the sin you are mourning has led you: sins of deception and pretense. Then consider what this sin of yours has cost others. Finally, think about how costly the sin you are mourning was for Jesus, as He bore your transgressions on the cross.

3. *Spiritual mourning arises from humility.* To develop heartfelt sorrow toward some attitude or action that has held (and may still hold) a powerful attraction, you must become poor in spirit, recalling your own inadequacy and recalling your sins as the motive for Christ's sacrifice. Seeing our sins as costly to Jesus takes us back to the first

Naming and recognizing the cost of your sins will lead you into spiritual mourning. Naming particular sins will focus your attention on what needs to change in your life, and counting the cost of these sins will press the urgency of change into your heart. Or, to use biblical language, naming your sins will show you where you need to repent, and counting their cost will bring you into the godly sorrow of repentance that leads to life.

When a person is bereaved, a wise counselor will often say, "Take time to grieve properly," and that advice is helpful when it comes to spiritual mourning. Naming and costing your sins will not be easy, but when this work is clearly and thoroughly done you will, by the grace of God, find that you are in a position to forsake the sin you have mourned.

two rings—naming our sins and feeling sorrow for our actions humbles us and gives us momentum to come before our God to confess and to depend on Him.

4. *Spiritual mourning is infused with hope.* When you mourn your sins, seeing them for what they are, it can be easy for you to despair. Instead remember that when God shines the light on your sins, His great purpose is to lead you to Jesus, the *friend* of sinners. In Him you will find hope. Hope is a signature mark of spiritual mourning, and it arises from faith in Christ and all that He has accomplished through the cross.

5. *Spiritual mourning happens at the cross.* True spiritual mourning always leads you to the cross. That is where you forsake these sins and break a pattern of habitual sin. Naming and confessing your sins will lead you into spiritual mourning, but knowing the love of Christ will take you further. And the love of Christ is always found at the foot of the cross.

6. *Spiritual mourning will lead you to forsake sins.* Spiritual mourning is the key to breaking sin's compulsive power. This is why we can speak of spiritual mourning as being a blessing. Do this work of spiritual mourning thoroughly, and you will have strength to overcome the sin that has defeated you, and to forsake it at the cross.

Godly sorrow *does* lead to repentance, and repentance *does* lead to life. When you see the connections, it soon becomes clear that cultivating the art of spiritual mourning is crucial to making progress in your Christian life.

3. Spiritual mourning arises from humility.

Spiritual mourning is a heartfelt sorrow over particular sins, *arising from humility* and infused with hope, that leads you to forsake these sins at the cross.

One major challenge in spiritual mourning is the difficulty of grieving over a sin that you have enjoyed.

Picture with me a person we will call Joe, who has come under the power of a habitual sin. It could be pride, anger, gossip, lust, drunkenness, or any other sin that has a habit-forming power. Over time, Joe's besetting sin has become increasingly compulsive. When he falls into it, Joe feels guilty. He tells God that he is sorry, but knowing the strength of this temptation in his life, he feels that it will not be long before he falls again.

Spiritual mourning seems to be beyond Joe's reach, because his sin brings him some degree of pleasure. The pleasure passes quickly, and he knows that it always leaves regret, but there is a comfort and pleasure for Joe in his sin of choice and that is why he keeps going back to it.

So how can Joe learn to hate what at least a part of him loves? How can he get to a place where he has *heartfelt sorrow* over something that has held a powerful attraction to him for so long? Joe sees that he needs to practice spiritual mourning, but how can he grieve over a sin that he loves?

One answer is that he becomes poor in spirit. Picture again those seven rings suspended between two platforms. How can you get on the second ring? Standing on the platform, it is beyond your reach and there's only one way to get there: you must take hold of the first ring and use the momentum of your swing to reach the second.

Let's apply this to Joe and the difficulty he has in getting onto the second ring of spiritual mourning. There is a way for Joe to make progress. If he swings on the first ring, the second will be within his reach. Seeing his poverty before God will get him started on mourning his sins.

Once you see this pattern of progress in the Beatitudes, you will know what to do at times when you feel stuck in your Christian life. Whenever one of the rings seems beyond your reach, go back and check out the rings that went before. Does peace of mind or purity of heart seem beyond you? Look at the rings that get you there. Go back to the beginning and use the momentum you will gain from each ring to move you forward.

4. Spiritual mourning is infused with hope.

Spiritual mourning is a heartfelt sorrow over particular sins, arising from humility and *infused with hope*, that leads you to forsake these sins at the cross.

When you mourn your sins, seeing them for what they are and taking in their cost, you need to know that you are in a place fraught with danger for your soul. It would be easy for you to despair, and you need to remember that when God shines the light on your sins, His great purpose is to lead you to Jesus, the friend of sinners, in whom you will find hope.

There is a kind of mourning over your sins and failures that locks you up in self-deprecation. Your eyes get focused on your own foolishness and failure, and your tears flow from bitter regret over missed opportunities and mess-ups. But there is no faith in that kind of mourning, and that is why it is ultimately destructive. Hope is a signature mark of spiritual mourning, and hope arises from faith in Christ and all that He has accomplished through the cross.

This can be seen in the final hours of Judas, who was seized with remorse after he betrayed our Lord. Judas grieved over what he had done. The Bible says that he "changed his mind" (Matt. 27:3), and his sincerity was evident in his returning the money that the chief priests had paid him for his act of betrayal. Judas looked at his sin with bitter regret, but he did not look to Christ for forgiveness and so his grief led him to despair.

The grief, regret, and despair of Judas is not spiritual mourning. It was another effect of him being consumed by the devil, who had entered into his heart. The Holy Spirit never leads a person to despair. He will lead you to mourn over your sins, but the mourning into which He leads you is always infused with hope.

This is why there are always two sides to the coin of genuine Christian experience. In spiritual mourning, a believer is "sorrowful, yet always rejoicing" (2 Cor. 6:10). Sorrowful because of the offense and the effect of our sins, and yet rejoicing in the hope that we see in Christ. Feeling your need, you will often find yourself saying, "Who is sufficient for these things?" (2 Cor. 2:16). But if your mourning is infused with hope, you will not stop there. You will go on to say, "Our sufficiency is from God" (2 Cor. 3:5).

The true Christian knows what it is to say with Paul, "I am the foremost" of sinners (1 Tim. 1:15). But if her mourning is infused with hope, she will also say, "But I received mercy . . . that in me . . . Jesus Christ might display his perfect patience" (v. 16). Or to put it in what is perhaps the best known expression of spiritual mourning in the Bible, you will often find yourself saying, "Wretched man that I am!" (Rom. 7:24) but looking to Christ, you will also be able to say, "Thanks be to God" (Rom. 7:25)!

So when you enter into spiritual mourning, make sure that while you have one eye fixed on your sin, your other eye is fixed on the cross. Robert Murray M'Cheyne advised one friend, "For every look at yourself, take ten looks at Christ." The context of that memorable line was the art of spiritual mourning. "Learn much of your own heart," M'Cheyne counseled his friend, "and when you have learned all you can, remember you have seen but a few yards into a pit that is unfathomable."[2]

The extent of our own sin, the effect of it, the depth of its root, and the pain of its consequence all threaten to overwhelm the believer who has taken an honest look into the murky depths of his or her own heart. So keep your eyes fixed on Christ when you go into spiritual mourning. Remember His grace and mercy, and trust in the power of His blood to cover and cleanse the worst and the most deeply rooted of sins.

5. Spiritual mourning happens at the cross.

Spiritual mourning is a heartfelt sorrow over particular sins, arising from humility and infused with hope, that leads you to forsake these sins *at the cross*.

We have been asking: How do you break a pattern of habitual sin? How can you enter into spiritual mourning in which you begin to hate what you used to love, and turn from what you used to choose?

We have identified several answers to these questions. You start by naming particular sins, and you proceed by counting their costs in terms of the price paid by yourself, by others, and by your Lord. You gain momentum in this process by seeing your need as one who stands empty-handed before almighty God. And you must have hope, because without it, your sorrow will lead you to shipwreck on the rocks of despair. All of this leads us to the cross, which is the venue for spiritual mourning.

Andrew Bonar was a godly Scottish pastor who kept an extraordinarily insightful journal of his own spiritual life. He struggled over why he did not hate sin more, why he fell back into the same sins, and how he could make more progress in overcoming them. In one entry to his diary, dated May 7, 1829, he wrote, "It has been much impressed upon me that, if convinced of sin at all, I must be so by the view of it in Christ's love."[3]

Naming and confessing your sins will lead you into spiritual mourning, but knowing the love of Christ will take you further. That was Bonar's experience, and in his ministry he helped people turn from their sins by showing them the love of Christ.

M'Cheyne, a close friend of Bonar, shared the same conviction. "It is commonly thought," he said, "that preaching the holy law is the most awakening truth in the Bible, that by it the mouth is stopped, and all the world becomes guilty before God; and indeed, I believe this is the most ordinary means which God makes use of. And yet to me there is something far more awakening in the sight of a Divine Savior freely offering Himself to every one of the human race."[4]

There's more in looking at the cross than seeing what your sin did to Jesus. The cross is about what Jesus did for you. At the cross you see how much you are loved, and that love will be the most convicting power of all. One glimpse of the love of Christ will do more to strengthen you in your battle against sin than any number of commitments or disciplines.

C. H. Spurgeon had a special gift of helping people who were prone to despair on account on their many sins and failures. He was sensitive toward the difficulty of people who knew the shallowness of their own repentance and felt that they were not sorry enough. His counsel was to show that spiritual mourning is not a sorrow that God calls us to manufacture in our hearts, but a gift that we receive from the hands of Jesus Christ. God is not calling you to work up repentance in order to offer it to Him; He invites you to come to Him so that you may find repentance at the cross.

Listen to how Spurgeon puts this:

Learn this lesson, not to trust Christ because you repent, but trust Christ to make you repent; not to come to Christ because you have a broken heart, but to come to him that he may give you a broken heart; not to come to him because you are fit to come, but to come to him because you are unfit to come. Your fitness is your unfitness. Your qualification is your *lack* of qualification.[5]

The point here is a simple one: all that we have said in this chapter is to be done at the cross. Naming your sin, recognizing its cost, gaining momentum in heartfelt sorrow, and finding hope that will keep you from despair all happens in the light of the Son of God who loved you and gave Himself for you. Draw near to Him, look at who He is and what He has done for you; take in His love for you, look at the mercy and the cleansing He offers to you, and think about the new heart He can give you. Look at your sin in the light of the cross and then ask Him to give you a heartfelt sorrow over the sin you are mourning that will enable you to forsake that sin at the cross.

6. Spiritual mourning will lead you to forsake sins.

Spiritual mourning is a heartfelt sorrow over particular sins, arising from humility and infused with hope, that leads you to *forsake these sins* at the cross.

I well remember when, as a teenager, I first grasped that repentance meant forsaking sin. I had gone to a conference in England where I heard Dr. Alan Redpath say, "God has not promised to forgive one sin that you are not willing to forsake." That went home to me. How could I possibly ask God to forgive me if I had no intention of quitting the sin I had just confessed? How could I come to God in confession if, in my heart, I expected to carry on doing the same thing?

Four decades later, these words remain with me: "God has not promised to forgive one sin that you are not willing to forsake!" Dr. Redpath was reflecting the truth of Isaiah 55:6–7 and of 2 Timothy 2:19 that we considered earlier: repentance means forsaking sin, and while it is true that in our weakness we may often find ourselves asking God to forgive a sin into which we have fallen many times, it remains the case that we cannot truly ask forgiveness without a serious intent of forsaking, in the strength that God provides, the sin that we confess.

When a sin has become habitual or when its repeated pattern has become engrained as an addiction, spiritual mourning will be your key to breaking its compulsive power, and it is for this reason that we can speak of the blessing of spiritual mourning. Do this work of spiritual mourning thoroughly and you will have strength to overcome the sin that has defeated you, and to forsake it at the cross.

"Blessed are the meek, for they shall inherit the earth."

MATTHEW 5:5

I GIVE
UP CONTROL

THE FREEDOM OF TOTAL SUBMISSION

What comes to your mind when you hear the word *meek*? Is a meek person someone who is soft-spoken? Or maybe someone with a limp handshake, or a person who does not have much spine?

One impression that comes to my mind is a hymn for children written by Charles Wesley: "Gentle Jesus." It begins, "Gentle Jesus, meek and mild, . . ." When you put *meek* and *mild* together, it gives the impression of being weak, limp, and lacking strength. I suspect that Wesley used "mild" because he was looking for a word that would rhyme with "child" and that's not easy to find! But "mild" gets us on the wrong track when it comes to meekness. A *mild* curry is not very strong, and probably not worth eating. To make matters worse, our English word "meekness" sounds suspiciously like "weakness," and if that's what it means, it doesn't sound like something we would want to pursue.

Yet in these beatitudes our Lord is telling us that there are some things of supreme value that we should go after at any cost, and one of them is meekness.

When I began to study this beatitude, I asked the question: What is Jesus referring to here? What is this *meekness* that I am to go after? That led me to a journey of discovery, in which I had to do a complete reset on the meaning of the word *meek* (which it turns out has nothing to do with weakness), and I found for the first time why meekness is crucial to making progress in the Christian life.

BECOMING "USED TO THE HAND"

I began my search with Matthew Henry, who wrote a book quaintly titled, *A Discourse on Meekness and Quietness of Spirit.* Henry points out that in Latin, a meek man was called *mansuetus.* There are two words here: *manu,* which means "hand," and *assuetus,* which means "used to." So *meekness* means being "used to the hand," which calls to mind the taming of a wild animal.

Think about a horse that has not yet been broken: it is not "used to the hand," and so when someone comes near it, the horse bucks and kicks. It resists the bit and bridle, and its strength is uncontrolled. But when the horse gets "used to the hand," its wild passions are subdued, its strength is brought under control, and the animal is at peace.

The Bible compares our fallen human nature to the impulse of wild animals. God says that His own people are like a wild donkey and a restless camel (Jer. 2:23–24). These are not flattering descriptions, but they are telling us something that we need to know: by nature, we are like wild animals. We have strength but it is neither directed nor controlled, and so our energy gets used in ways that are at best unproductive and at worst destructive. If we want to become useful to God, we need to get "used to the hand." When that happens, your wild passions will be subdued, your strength will be harnessed, and you will begin to experience peace.

Meekness is controlled strength. It tames the temper, subdues the self, calms the passions, manages the impulses of the heart, and brings order out of chaos in the soul. When I saw this, my interest was engaged. If this is meekness, I want to get as much of it as I possibly can.

A person characterized by meekness is humble, gentle, patient, forgiving, and content. Meekness is the means by which God delivers us from pride, harshness, aggression, vengeance, and turmoil. Think about someone in your life who might be described as self-opinionated and overbearing. He throws his weight around, is short-tempered and demanding, and always insists on his own way. The man is not happy. There is turmoil inside him, and it spills out over other people. If this man were to get "used to the hand" it would change his temper and subdue his passions, giving him a new dignity, poise, and peace. That's the power of meekness.

Jesus is calling us to something very wonderful here. Think about what controlled strength could mean in your life. Growing in meekness will subdue your impulsiveness, giving you control over anger. It will change the way you speak, giving you control over the harsh word and the sharp put-down. Growing in meekness will lead you into contentment, bringing you peace as you get used to the hand of God even in the difficult circumstances of your life. Most of all, growing in meekness will position you to be useful in God's service.

MEEKNESS COMES THROUGH SUBMITTING

Meekness is strength brought under control *through submission.* Think about the wild horse becoming "used to the hand." Its strength comes under control as it *submits* to the bit and bridle. Our English word "submission" is, again, a combination of two words; "mission" and "sub." So submission means you put your *mission* under (*sub*) the mission of something or someone else.

When I first spoke about meekness in the church that I serve, a thoughtful and insightful woman came to speak with me after the service. "I have always been a really competitive person," she said. "I was competitive in sports and I have been the same in business. So the whole idea of submission has been difficult for me, but your analogy of taming the wild horse has helped me and here's why: it's only when the horse submits to the bit and bridle that it can have any chance of winning the race! I want to win, and for the first time, I've seen that winning is only possible when my strength is brought under control, and that happens through submission."

She had a marvelous insight. Wild horses don't win races. Winning begins when your strength is brought under control by submission to Jesus Christ. But what does this look like in practice? To answer that question, we need to fill out our definition of meekness. Meekness is controlled strength that comes through submission *to God's Word, God's will, and God's people.*

Submitting to God's Word

Meekness involves submitting to God's Word. The apostle James wrote, "Receive with meekness the implanted word, which is able to save your souls" (1:21). To receive God's Word with meekness means that you place yourself under the authority of Scripture, allowing God to shape what you believe and direct what you do through the Bible.

I am grateful for the privilege of serving a church where the Bible is highly valued. That was true long before I came and I trust that it will be true long after I am gone. A church where the Bible is highly valued and clearly taught is a wonderful place to be because it is through the Word that our lives are nourished and we grow. But such a church is also a *dangerous* place to be, because we are all responsible for putting what we hear into practice.

Do you receive God's Word with meekness? Are you submitting yourself to the Scriptures, allowing God to bend and reshape your beliefs, desires, and affections in the light of His commands and His promises?

That can be a challenge. The self-willed person hears what God says in the Bible, but reserves the right to disagree: "God may say that, but I don't believe it." Or, "God may say that, but I'm not yet ready to move in that direction." Or worse, "What I want must be what God says."

Meekness will make you flexible under the shaping influence of God's Word. Your life will become like soft wax in which the Word of God makes a visible and lasting imprint.

Submitting to God's Will

Meekness involves submitting to God's will. There will be times in your life when God puts you in a place that you would not have chosen. It may come through difficult circumstances at work, in your family, at church, or in regards to your health. What does it mean *then* for your strength to be brought under control as you submit yourself to Him?

Come with me to a garden called Gethsemane. It's late and it's dark, and three men are asleep on the ground. Further on, there is another man. Drawing near to Him, you see that the man's upper body is draped over a large stone. He is sweating profusely, and in an agony of soul He cries out, "'Father, if it be possible, let this cup pass from me; nevertheless, not as I will, but as you will'" (Matt. 26:39).

Frame that picture and give it the title "Meekness." This is meekness in its essence: Jesus Christ submitting Himself to the will of the Father at unimaginable cost—death by crucifixion! And to this path of submission, Christ now calls us when He says, "Blessed are the meek, for they shall inherit the earth."

Submitting to God's People

Meekness, which brings strength under control, is practiced by submitting to God's Word and His will. But there is another dimension to this, as God calls us to submit to His people (Eph. 5:21). If you thought submission to God's Word and will would be hard, submission to God's people may prove to be even harder, but this too is the will of God, and this is where true blessing will be found.

In Ephesians 5, Paul describes what it looks like when God's people are filled with the Holy Spirit. The first and most immediate evidence is that God's people are filled with joy and sing to each other in psalms, hymns, and spiritual songs (v. 19). A second evidence is that they are overwhelmingly thankful (v. 20). But there is a third evidence that is especially important for us here: "submitting to one another out of reverence for Christ" (v. 21). This is a distinguishing mark of people who are filled with the Holy Spirit.

In our Western culture, independent, autonomous, self-directed, and disconnected Christians often enjoy floating between churches, sampling the best without committing to any. But to whom does a person submit if he or she is not a member of a local church? How can you obey the command of God in Ephesians 5:21 if you have not committed yourself clearly and publicly to a gathered community of believers? I've heard Christians say that they are accountable to a small group, but a small group is not a church, and there is a big difference between a group of friends chosen by you and a congregation gathered by God.

Meekness grows through the discipline of committed relationships in the body of Christ. In a world of rampant individualism, this is a serious question: how can you submit to other believers, as God commands, if you are not a committed member of a local church?

Meekness comes into play in the church when you don't get your way, or when a decision is not to your liking. Your first impulse in that circumstance may be to walk away from your brothers and sisters in Christ. But God calls you to submit to them. It takes real strength to do that, but when you do, you will grow in the blessing of meekness.

But how can you practice submission if the pattern of your life is to walk away when other Christians upset or disappoint you? Meekness will grow as you choose to submit yourself to others when you do not get your own way.

Limits in Submitting to God's People

There is an important distinction to be made between our submission to God and our submission to His people. We always submit to God. God never submits to us. But submission among God's people moves in two directions. We are to submit *to one another* and, at different times, this will involve both giving and receiving.

Another distinction is that there are no limits or boundaries in our submission to God's Word and His will, but there are limits in our submission to God's people. The apostles said, "We must obey God rather than men" (Acts 5:29), and there may be times when we have to say that too. But remember, the apostles took this stand when they were forbidden to preach the gospel, so the circumstances that might cause us to invoke the Acts 5:29 principle would be unusual to say the least. The normal pattern of healthy Christian relationships is that we submit to one other in the body of Christ.

Listen to how Paul puts this in writing to the church at Philippi: "Do nothing from selfish ambition or conceit, but in humility count others more significant than yourselves" (Phil. 2:3). This means I must listen to what others are saying and give weight to what others think, especially when I feel sure that I am right and that they are mistaken.

Meekness in Christian Ministry

Meekness is a distinctive of Christian character and a defining mark of Christian ministry. The word translated as "meek" in the third beatitude is sometimes rendered "gentle," and it is used in relation to teaching, witness, and discipline in the church.

Christian preaching is to be characterized by meekness. In 2 Timothy 2:24–25 Paul says, "The Lord's servant must not be quarrelsome but kind to everyone, able to teach, patiently enduring evil, correcting his opponents with gentleness." In other words, the ministry of the Word that guides the church is to be given with controlled strength or meekness. Christian preaching is not to be characterized by thumping authoritarianism, but by a humble and gentle spirit.

The same character that is to be displayed within the church by its leaders is also to be shown in the world by its members. The apostle Peter says, "Always [be] prepared to make a defense to anyone who asks you for a reason for the hope that is in you; yet do it with *gentleness* and respect" (1 Peter 3:15, emphasis added). There is no place for bombastic or condescending Christian witness. We are to bear witness to Christ in the spirit of meekness, showing respect to others because we know ourselves to be people who hang on to the grace and the mercy of God.

This same spirit of meekness shows up again in Galatians 6:1, where Paul describes a situation in which someone is "caught" (literally "trapped") in a sin. When that happens, spiritually mature people should restore the person who has been trapped, but they must do this in a spirit of meekness, knowing that the same impulse to sin that trapped the one who has fallen lives in their own flesh as well.

Meekness is emphasized repeatedly in the New Testament in relation to both Christian character and ministry. We are to go after meekness and develop it in our ministries as much as possible.

MEN OF MEEKNESS

Having established a definition and given a description, it is time to hone in on what meekness looks like in practice, and for this purpose we will consider four examples taken from the lives of Moses, David, Paul, and Jesus.

Moses: Meekness When You Are Opposed

The starting place for any cameo of meekness must be Moses. Scripture tells us that "Moses was very meek, more than all people who were on the face of the earth" (Num. 12:3). Nobody in Old Testament times modeled controlled strength more than Moses. He was the supreme example of meekness.

Think for a moment about what Moses had to endure: God called this man out of retirement to lead the people of Israel, who had been slaves for four hundred years, into freedom. The task was overwhelming and it was fraught with difficulty and danger.

By God's grace, Moses led God's people out of slavery in Egypt. It was Moses who stretched his hand over the sea to divide the waters (Ex. 14:16). It was Moses who threw a log into the bitter waters at Marah, turning them sweet so that the people could drink in the desert, and through Moses God announced the miraculous provision of food for the people.

You might think that God's people would be grateful. Instead they complained bitterly against Moses. The man who had brought them so much blessing became the focus of their bitter complaint: "Why did you bring us up out of Egypt, to kill us and our children . . . with thirst?" (Ex. 17:3). Really? Can you imagine God's people believing this about Moses?

Actually it was worse, because Moses cried to the Lord, "What shall I do with this people? They are almost ready to stone me" (v. 4). After all that Moses had done for them, God's people were thinking about killing him.

I've tried to put myself in Moses's sandals, and I can well imagine my impulse to say, "Listen up, people. All I hear from you is moaning and complaining about what you don't like! The truth is that you have never seen such blessing as you are experiencing right now, and if you can't see that, I am out of here!" But Moses was different. He was meek.

Instead of lashing out at these ungrateful people, he prayed for them and continued to serve them, and on one occasion even said to God that he was ready to lay down his life for them (Ex. 32:32). That's meekness. Far from being a form of weakness, it is strength under control that was formed in Moses through his complete submission to God.

Think about a situation in which someone who should be grateful to you has begun to complain against you. You have tried to do them good but they assume the worst about you and mutter behind your back. Most leaders know what this is like. It is always frustrating, sometimes exasperating, and at its worst can be devastating. Having stood in the sandals of Moses, I can see why God described him as the meekest man "on the face of the earth" (Num. 12:3). He modeled "sub"-"mission" by giving himself to the purpose of God, and he remains the supreme Old Testament example of controlled strength and continued commitment in the face of discouragement and opposition.

David: Meekness When You Are Provoked

If there is someone in your life who exasperates you, spare a thought for King David, who endured the incorrigible antics of Shimei. This man belonged to the house of Saul, and he had nothing good to say about David, even though David had been anointed by God, and Saul (the former king) was long since dead.

Shimei was a thorn in David's side. He cursed continually, and he even threw stones at David (2 Sam. 16:5–7). Can you imagine this? Throwing stones at the king of Israel! When David traveled in public he endured the insult of this wretched man running after him and shouting, "Get out, get out, you man of blood, you worthless man!" (2 Sam. 16:7). Abishai, who was one of David's loyal men, didn't think the king should have to put up with this: "Why should this dead dog curse my lord the king? Let me go over and take off his head" (v. 9).

Put yourself in David's sandals. What would you have said to Abishai?

It would have been easy for David to say, "Good idea, Abishai. Let's be done with this." But David showed meekness toward Shimei: "Leave him alone," he said, "and let him curse" (16:11). And, of course, that is what Shimei proceeded to do. Try to picture this scene as it is described in the Scriptures: "David and his men went on the road, while Shimei went along on the hillside opposite him and cursed as he went and threw stones at him and flung dust. And the king, and all the people who were with him, arrived weary at the Jordan" (2 Sam. 16:13–14).

Shimei exhibited extreme, unjustifiable provocation toward the king of Israel, and David put up with it. The journey to Jordan must have been a miserable one, and when the king and his companions finally arrived they were exhausted, and presumably covered in the dust that Shimei had thrown down on them from the hillside.

Think about how David putting up with Shimei reflects the patience, meekness, and kindness of God. David had at his disposal all the power of the loyal men who surrounded him. With a simple command, he could have put an end to Shimei and his foolish antics, but he demonstrated meekness—controlled strength—in the face of extreme provocation.

How much more can this be said of God in relation to us. "How easily God could crush sinners, and kick them into hell," Thomas Watson wrote. "But he moderates his anger."[1] God puts up with us when we dishonor Him. Even when He is provoked, He restrains the judgment that would crush us. That is meekness: controlled strength, and more than that, strength that is deployed in the great mission of God, which is not to crush and destroy but, by His grace, to save and redeem.

So think about a situation in which you are provoked. Perhaps there is a person who does not show you due respect, or someone who, for no obvious reason, seems to have set himself or herself against you. If

God were to remove this person, your life would be much easier, but for some reason He has allowed this person to remain in your life. Through their exasperating antics, God is calling you to grow in meekness.

Paul: Meekness When You Are Disappointed

You may also be called to exercise meekness especially when other people let you down. The apostle Paul extended himself in the cause of church planting and endured extraordinary hardships for the sake of others who found Christ through his ministry.

Like all of us, Paul needed the prayers, help, and encouragement of other believers, and it is for this reason that he often asked for these things in his letters. Sometimes he was greatly blessed by the kindness of his brothers and sisters in Christ, but there were also times when other Christians let him down. One of these times came after his arrest. To Paul's evident surprise and disappointment, when his trial began, none of the local believers showed up.

"At my first defense no one came to stand by me, but all deserted me" (2 Tim. 4:16). After all that Paul had poured into the lives of so many believers, it was reasonable for him to expect that someone would show up in the courtroom. But standing in the dock, he looked around for a friendly face and found none.

Perhaps there has been a time when you were let down by people you thought would be there for you. You invested in relationships, extended yourself for others, but when you were in need yourself, the kindness was not returned.

Disappointment is a seedbed for bitterness, and when other people let you down, it is easy for a cancer to take root in your soul. But far from becoming bitter, Paul gives us a marvelous example of meekness in the face of disappointment: "At my first defense no one came to stand by me, but all deserted me. May it not be charged against them!" (2 Tim. 4:16). There's honesty about the disappointment but no recrimination.

Think about how this works in relation to marriage. When two sinners, both in the process of redemption, commit to share their whole lives together, there are going to be some challenges for sure. What else would you expect? God remembers that your spouse is dust, and if you follow Him in remembering this too, you will grow in meekness. This will also help you in parenting your children. God remembers the frailty of our children, and when wise parents follow this example, it delivers us from imposing unrealistic expectations.

I find that thinking about the burdens that other people carry helps me here. You never know the strength of another person's temptation. If you were able to stand in the shoes of a brother, and feel the strength of a particular temptation as he experiences it in his life, you might come to the conclusion that he is doing better in the battle than you would have done.

Matthew Henry says, "The consideration of the common infirmity and corruption of mankind should be made use of, not to excuse our own faults . . . but to excuse the faults of others."[3] If I apply the truth that every Christian is a sinner in the process of redemption correctly, I will moderate my expectations of others, and grow in meekness.

2. Find joy in evidences of God's grace.

Finally, brothers, whatever is true, whatever is honorable, whatever is just, whatever is pure, whatever is lovely, whatever is commendable, if there is any excellence, if there is anything worthy of praise, think about these things.
—Philippians 4:8

Thinking about what is commendable and worthy of praise is huge for overcoming anger, frustration, and disappointment. The principle contained in this verse is so important for the promotion of meekness that there have been seasons in my own life when I have spoken this verse aloud to myself every single day.

Picture a new housing development in which the homes being built are all at different stages of development. In some, the walls are up, the roof is on, and you can already imagine what the finished homes will look like. "These are going to be great," you say. But others are only holes in the ground, surrounded by mud, and you wonder, "Will these ever amount to anything?"

Christians are like houses at different stages of development. In some you can see the forming and shaping of a reflection of Jesus Christ. In others, the work has hardly begun, and what you see may be as discouraging as a bare hole in the ground. But at least there's a hole! God is digging a foundation. Rejoice in that! A beginning has been made and there is reason for joy in every stage of progress.

Find joy in what God is doing in the lives of others. Learn to admire even small evidences of the grace of God in them, and remember that any faith, hope, or love is a work of God's Spirit. None of us is yet what we will be but, in Christ, all of us will one day be complete.

3. Remember how much you have been forgiven.

Whoever lacks these qualities is so nearsighted that he is blind, having forgotten that he was cleansed from his former sins. —2 Peter 1:9

When Peter lists the marks of a growing walk with Jesus Christ, he speaks about self-control, steadfastness, and love (vv. 6–7). Strength under control brings us to the world of meekness. Then Peter tells us that a person who does not have this has "forgotten that he was cleansed from his former sins." It follows that if you remember how much you have been forgiven, you will grow in meekness.

Again Matthew Henry is helpful in suggesting that we ask this question: "If God should be as angry with me for every provocation as I am with those about me, what would become of me?"[4] When you know that you have been forgiven much, you will love much. Remember how much you have been forgiven and you will grow in meekness.

4. Take time before you form judgments.

Let every person be quick to hear, slow to speak, slow to anger. —James 1:19

You probably know, as I do, what it is to say something on impulse and then to wish you had not spoken so quickly. David knew this too, and he confessed the sin of jumping to harsh conclusions about other people: "I said in my haste, All men are liars" (Ps. 116:11 KJV). In the book of Proverbs, Solomon reminds us that "the one who states his case first seems right, until the other comes and examines him" (18:17). You know what this is like: you hear a story and it seems right until you hear the other side, and then you wish you hadn't been so quick to form an opinion.

Describing the person who easily gets worked up, Spurgeon says, "Little pots soon boil over." Some people are like that. As soon as they hear a piece of gossip, they boil over with indignation. They make immediate judgments without even knowing if a thing is true. Don't be a little pot that soon boils over. Be quick to hear, but slow to speak and very slow to anger. Take time before you form judgments. It will help you grow in meekness.

5. Make friends with meek people.

Make no friendship with a man given to anger . . . lest you learn his ways and entangle yourself in a snare. —Proverbs 22:24–25

Did you know that the Bible says you should not make friends with a person who is given to anger? It's a direct command from God! If a person is habitually angry, he or she is not the friend for you, and

87

here's why: "Lest you learn his ways." If you choose the company and conversation of a person who is constantly complaining, and whose pattern is to be angry about one issue and then about another, the habit of his or her heart will eventually rub off on you.

You may have to work with people who are habitually angry, but God tells you not to choose them as your friends. Choose instead to make friends with meek people. Cultivate the company of those whose

GAINING MOMENTUM / Ten Strategies for Cultivating Meekness

1. *Moderate your expectations of others.* God remembers your frailty (Ps. 103:14), and you should remember the frailty of others. Doing so will moderate your expectations of people. If you apply the truth that every Christian is a sinner in the process of redemption correctly, you will moderate your expectations of others, and grow in meekness.

2. *Find joy in evidences of God's grace.* Find joy in what God is doing in the lives of others. Learn to admire even small evidences of the grace of God in them. Remember that any faith, hope, or love is a work of God's Spirit.

3. *Remember how much you have been forgiven.* Sometimes we forget our own status as sinners saved by Jesus' sacrifice. The apostle Peter tells us that a person who does not have such qualities as self-control, steadfastness, and love has "forgotten that he was cleansed from his former sins" (2 Peter 1:6–7, 9). It follows that if you remember how much you have been forgiven, you will grow in meekness.

4. *Take time before you form judgments.* Avoid the sin of jumping to harsh conclusions about other people. Be quick to hear, but slow to speak and very slow to anger. Take time before you form judgments. It will help you grow in meekness.

5. *Make friends with meek people.* God tells you not to choose angry people as your friends, "lest you learn [their] ways and entangle yourself in a snare" (Prov. 22:25). Instead, seek the company of those whose words and actions are under control. Making friends with people who are meek will help you to grow in meekness.

words and actions are under control. Making friends with people who are meek will help you to grow in meekness.

6. Take pleasure in the joys and successes of others.

Rejoice with those who rejoice, weep with those who weep. —Romans 12:15

I wonder which of these two responses you think would be the greater challenge. There's little doubt in my mind. It is often easier to

6. *Take pleasure in the joys and successes of others.* Meekness rejoices with those who rejoice, so when you see someone who is more blessed than you, thank God for their blessing. Grow in meekness and you will overcome the impulses of envy and self-interest that otherwise would wreak havoc in your soul.

7. *Discern God's hand in the work of your enemies.* If you see your life as a story of what others have done to you, you will live in disappointment, frustration, and resentment. But in Jesus you see something completely different: a Son who in meekness accepted God's good and perfect plan, even when enemies attacked. God also has a good and perfect plan for you and me when we come under attack.

8. *Walk in daily fellowship with Jesus Christ.* Meekness is embodied in Jesus, and we learn meekness as we yoke ourselves to Him. We are not born with a meek and gentle nature; it is a virtue we must learn, and we learn it from Jesus. You will grow in meekness as you bind yourself to the Savior and walk with Him.

9. *Anticipate all that God has promised.* A great inheritance that can never perish is "kept in heaven for you" (1 Peter 1:4). When God creates a new heaven and a new earth, He will give it to the meek. You can be at peace when power has been seized by those who should not have it because you know that the meek will inherit the earth.

10. *Ask God to give you meekness.* We are to ask God for wisdom, writes the apostle James, and recognize that the wisdom God gives "is first pure, then peaceable, *gentle* . . ." (James 1:5; 3:17). When you ask God to help you grow in meekness, you can be confident that He will hear and answer your prayer.

share other people's sorrows than it is to enter into other people's joys.

Spurgeon endured multiple illnesses during his life and sometimes was laid aside from the work that he loved. Friends would visit when he was ill and Spurgeon picked up on a rather unhelpful comment that some of his visitors would make: "Sometimes, when I am ill, someone comes in and says, 'I have been to see somebody who is worse than you are.'"

The point of this often repeated comment is, of course, to make the sick person feel better by knowing that others are worse. But Spurgeon said, "I never get any comfort out of such a remark, and my usual answer is, 'You have made me feel worse than I was before by telling me that there is somebody worse even than I am.'"[5]

Spurgeon then pointed out that the great comfort for a meek person is not to know that others are worse but that others are doing better: "The meek spirited man is glad to know that other people are happy, and *their* happiness is *his* happiness."[6]

Think with me about this: meekness means you are glad for others who have more than you. When was the last time you heard a person say: "I don't have much money but at least I have the joy of knowing that other people have more"? "My health is poor but at least other people are well, so thank God for that"? "My son is really struggling right now, but at least my friend's children are doing well"? We don't often say these things, but perhaps that is because meekness is hard and there's not much of it about.

Meekness rejoices with those who rejoice, so when you see someone who is more blessed than you, thank God for their blessing. Grow in meekness and you will overcome the impulses of envy and self-interest that otherwise would wreak havoc in your soul.

7. Discern God's hand in the work of your enemies.

"Shall I not drink the cup that the Father has given me?" —John 18:11

Thomas Watson asks, "What made Christ so meek in His sufferings?"

His answer: "He did not look at Judas or Pilate, but at his Father."[7]

At one level, you could say that the suffering of Jesus on the cross was a direct result of Judas betraying Him and of Pilate condemning Him. On the cross, our Lord could have said, "Look at what Judas has done to me!" or "Look at the injustice I have suffered at the hands of Pilate." But Christ did not do that. He looked instead to His Father, and discerning the hand of God, even in the work of His enemies, He viewed His suffering as "the cup that *the Father* has given me."

If you see your life as a story of what others have done to you, you will live in disappointment, anger, frustration, and resentment. But in Jesus you see something completely different: after all that His enemies did to Him, He speaks with the controlled strength of meekness and says, "Father forgive them, they do not know what they are doing." And He was able to do this because He looked not at Judas or Pilate, but at His Father.

8. Walk in daily fellowship with Jesus Christ.

"Take my yoke upon you, and learn from me, for I am gentle and lowly in heart, and you will find rest for your souls." —Matthew 11:29

Jesus Christ is gentle. Meekness is embodied in Him, and we learn meekness as we yoke ourselves to Him. A yoke joins two animals so that they can pull the plow together as they walk side by side. Jesus says, "Yoke yourself to Me. Walk with Me, and learn from Me."

No one is born meek. Watson says, "By nature, the heart is like a troubled sea, casting forth the foam of anger and wrath."[8] So meekness

91

is a virtue we must learn, and we learn it from Jesus. You will grow in meekness as you bind yourself to the Savior and walk with Him.

9. Anticipate all that God has promised.

"Blessed are the meek, for they shall inherit the earth." —Matthew 5:5

Inherit is a wonderful word. It speaks of a relationship in which something that belongs to someone else is willed, by their kindness, to you.

When God adopted you into His family, He also placed you in His will. That's why Peter said you have an inheritance that can never perish and never fade, "kept in heaven for you" (1 Peter 1:4). When God creates a new heaven and a new earth, He will give it to the meek.

In the third beatitude, our Lord was quoting from Psalm 37:11, where David says, "The meek shall inherit the land." At the time of Jesus, the Promised Land was not in the hands of the meek but in the hands of the mighty, as God's people were crushed under the iron fist of Rome. All of the power was on the other side, and some felt that God's people should fight fire with fire. But the land will not be possessed by zealous believers thrashing around like unbroken horses. Christ calls His people to a calm poise, to a reasoned spirit, and to the controlled strength of meekness.

It surely is significant that the psalm in which David says that the meek will inherit the land begins by saying, "Fret not yourself because of evildoers. . . . For they will soon fade like the grass" (Ps. 37:1–2). You can be at peace when power has been seized by those who should not have it because you know that the meek will inherit the earth.

Try to take in the glory of your inheritance! "All things are yours, and you are Christ's and Christ is God's" (1 Cor. 3:21, 23). Grasp this and you will be released from envy, fear, anger, self-pity, and resentment.

John Calvin makes the point beautifully: "Let us be clear about this: provided, as he [Christ] says, we exercise self-control and are patient, provided we possess that gentleness which he requires of us and to which he calls us, we will inherit the whole earth."[9]

10. Ask God to give you meekness.

If any of you lacks wisdom, let him ask God, who gives generously to all without reproach, and it will be given him. —James 1:5

James speaks of asking God for wisdom and then he describes the wisdom that God gives: "The wisdom from above is first pure, then peaceable, *gentle*, open to reason, full of mercy and good fruits" (James 3:17, emphasis added).

When you ask God to help you grow in meekness, you can be confident that He will hear and answer your prayer. So come to Him and ask: "Lord, You have said that a gentle and quiet spirit is of great worth in Your sight. Please give me that spirit. Help me to curb this harsh tongue. Keep me from rash judgments, and help me to think the best of others. Open my eyes to discern Your hand at work even when I face great difficulties. Help me to find pleasure in the joy of others, and so to walk with Christ that a reflection of Your meek Son, Jesus, may be formed in me today."

"*Blessed are those who hunger and thirst for righteousness, for they shall be satisfied.*"

MATTHEW 5:6

4

I LONG TO
BE RIGHTEOUS

THE ENERGY OF RENEWED AFFECTIONS

We have reached a turning point. So far, we have learned that the blessed person is one who becomes poor in spirit, mourns over his or her sins, and submits to the will of God. The first three beatitudes all deal with our need. They humble us and lead us to bow before God with penitent and teachable hearts.

The fourth beatitude is about the desire that arises from such a heart. Out of the blessings found in the first three beatitudes comes the greater blessing of a heart that truly hungers and thirsts for God and for righteousness. If you have ever wondered how to foster a stronger desire for holiness in your life, the answer is right here before you.

The church I serve is called The Orchard, and we often speak there about roots, life, and fruit. The analogy is a helpful one. Spiritual life begins when God brings new life through the living seed of His Word planted in the soul (1 Peter 1:21). We encourage people to put down deep roots into the Scriptures, knowing that a healthy plant draws life through its roots, and that fruit will be formed as the roots continue to nourish the plant.

I'm convinced that there is a roots-life-fruit pattern to the Beatitudes: the first three beatitudes form the roots of a godly life, and since these roots lie in an awareness of our own need, they produce a deep longing for what we do not have. Becoming poor in spirit, mourning over your sins, and submitting your life to God will produce a deep hunger and thirst for righteousness in your soul. This desire is the life of godliness, and it will produce the beautiful fruit of mercy, purity, and peace that Christ speaks of in the fifth, sixth, and seventh beatitudes.

TWO KINDS OF RIGHTEOUSNESS

The Righteousness God Gives You

The Bible speaks of righteousness in two distinct ways, and it is important to distinguish between them. First, there is the righteousness that Christ *gives* you. Christ is our righteousness (1 Cor. 1:30). That means that the righteousness on which we depend is in Him and not in us. Christ lived the fully righteous life that we have failed to live, even at our Christian best. He laid down this perfect life as a sacrifice for our sins and now offers His righteousness to all who will trust in Him. When, by faith, we are united to Christ, God counts us as righteous in Him. This marvelous gift is sometimes referred to as "imputed righteousness," which simply means righteousness that belongs to another being counted as ours.

The apostle Paul speaks of this imputed righteousness when he says that he wants to be found in Christ, "not having a righteousness of my own that comes from the law, but that which comes through faith in Christ, the righteousness from God that depends on faith" (Phil. 3:9). At the heart of Paul's conversion to Christ was a change in his understanding of righteousness. Before he met Christ, he thought he had it, but when he encountered the risen Lord, he knew for sure that he was far from righteous, and that his only hope lay in receiving a righteousness that he did not have.

The Righteousness God Calls You To

But along with the righteousness that Christ gives you, the Bible also speaks of a righteousness to which He calls you. This is what Jesus was referring to when He spoke about hungering and thirsting for righteousness.

If someone asked you, "Why did Jesus die?" you could give several answers that would be faithful to the Bible. For example, Christ died so that we might be forgiven; He died so that we might have eternal life. But consider the answer given by the apostle Peter: "He himself bore our sins in his body on the tree, that we might die to sin and *live to righteousness*" (1 Peter 2:24, emphasis added). The same outcome is laid out in Romans 8, where Paul tells us that God sent His Son and condemned sin in the flesh (a marvelous reference to what Christ accomplished for us on the cross) "in order that the *righteous requirement of the law might be fulfilled in us, who walk not according to the flesh but according to the Spirit*" (Rom. 8:4, emphasis added).

The purpose of the passion of Jesus is that we should have a passion for the pursuit of righteousness. Christ died to redeem a people who no longer live for themselves but who live with a deep desire to pursue holiness, which is a distinguishing mark of every Christian.

The difference between the righteousness that Christ gives us and the righteousness to which He calls us is important to grasp. People who come to Christ in penitent faith realize that they don't have what it takes before God. That is why we come, and when we do, we receive the marvelous gift of Christ's perfect righteousness, draped over us and counted by God as if it were our own. Since Christ gives this righteousness fully and freely to all who trust in Him, no Christian need ever hunger and thirst after it. Who hungers for what he already has? The righteousness of Christ is a gift to be treasured, not a virtue to be sought.

But to all who are in Christ, God gives His Holy Spirit, who renews our hearts and creates within us a new and deep desire to live in a way that is pleasing to Him. Christ's people hunger and thirst for righteousness, because while we know that we are forgiven and accepted before God on the basis of all that Christ is and all that He has done, we also know how far we are from all that Christ calls us to be.

At the same time, Christians are fully righteous and hungry for righteousness—and there is no contradiction between these two realities. A. W. Tozer said that "we have been snared in the coils of a spurious logic which insists that if we have found God, we need no more seek him."[1] Adapting that thought, we could say that we have been snared in the coils of a spurious logic that insists if we are righteous in Christ we need no longer hunger and thirst for righteousness. But Jesus calls us to this, and the distinguishing mark of those who are righteous in Christ is that they long for righteousness.

OBSERVATIONS ABOUT HUNGER

"Blessed are those who hunger and thirst
for righteousness, for they shall be satisfied."
(Matthew 5:6, emphasis added)

Hunger is a sign of need.

Hunger is a sign of need. When you are hungry, your body is telling you something: it's been too long since your last meal and you need to eat. Hunger indicates the *absence* of food in the body. It is the body's awareness of its own need.

Jesus tells us that the ones who are blessed are those who *hunger and thirst* for righteousness. The blessing belongs not to those who think that they are righteous, but to those who see how far they have to go. It rests not on those who remain content in their sins but on those who have a strong desire to extend themselves in the pursuit of a life that is pleasing to God.

The mark of a true Christian is not that she feels righteous, but that she longs to be more righteous than she is. When it comes to righteousness, the blessed people are not those who think they have it, but those who feel their need of it. That's good news for us, because the first three beatitudes have convinced us of our need and brought us to the place where we long to grow in righteousness.

Aren't you glad that Jesus did *not* say: "Blessed are the righteous, for they will be satisfied"? Where would that leave us? The blessing would *never* be ours because, as we have seen, we are far from righteous. Thank God He said, "Blessed are those who *hunger and thirst* for righteousness." It is not the realization of the desire, but *the desire itself* that Christ pronounces blessed.

Hunger is a sign of life and spiritual health.

Hunger is a sign of life and health. Nobody teaches a newborn baby how to be hungry. They don't need mentoring on this. Where there's life, there's hunger. Spurgeon said, "To hunger after righteousness is a sign of spiritual life. Nobody who was spiritually dead ever did this. . . . If you hunger and thirst after righteousness, you are spiritually alive."[2]

Losing your appetite may be a sign of illness, but when your appetite returns it is usually a sign of recovery. In the same way, knowing that you need to grow in Christ, and thirsting to be more like Him, is a sure sign of spiritual health. When it comes to the pursuit of righteousness, true Christians never feel they have arrived; they always long for more.

Alexander Maclaren says, "There is a great deal more in Christianity than longing, but there is no Christianity worth the name without it."[3]

Tozer wrote powerfully about thirsting for God:

> The whole transaction of religious conversion has been made mechanical and spiritless. Faith may now be exercised without a jar to the moral life and without embarrassment to the Adamic ego. Christ may be "received" without creating any special love for him in the soul of the receiver. The man is "saved" but he is not hungry or thirsty after God.[4]

Returning to this theme some years later, Tozer wrote, "Present day evangelical Christianity is not producing saints. . . . God is valued as being useful and Christ appreciated because of the predicaments he gets us out of. He can deliver us from the consequences of our past, relax our nerves, give us peace of mind and make our business a success. The all-consuming love that burns . . . is foreign to the modern religious spirit."[5]

Tozer believed that the self-satisfied Christianity that was growing in his time was toxic and that if it prevailed, it would bring devastating effects in the long term. "A widespread revival of the kind of Christianity we know today might prove to be a moral tragedy from which we would not recover in a hundred years."[6] Tozer's words have proved prophetic. In the fifty-plus years that have followed his death in 1963, the emaciated Christianity he described has multiplied in America, and now we are seeing the moral tragedy of which he spoke sweeping across our country. We desperately need to rediscover the mighty longing after God of which Tozer so eloquently spoke.

Hunger is a powerful motivation.

Hunger is more than a vague interest—it is an intense desire. A person who is really hungry will do almost anything to get food. His life depends on it.

Hunger is the strongest of motives. It produces energy and it drives decisive action that will make a difference not only at home and at church but also in the world of work.

Think about the professions in which many people serve: banking, law, teaching, finance, medicine, construction, manufacturing, insurance, and property development. Each of these professions has its own world of complexity that gives rise to a long list of ethical questions. Where are the boundaries between legitimate competition and destructive aggression? Where is the line between using the systems of your profession and manipulating them? Where is the line between appropriate reward and raw self-interest?

In any line of business there are people who need to be restrained, lest they exploit others, and so in every profession we have ever-increasing regulation. Policies, processes, and procedures are produced to make sure that people behave in an ethical manner, but every law that is passed has loopholes, and human ingenuity will always find them.

Regulation brings restraint, but it cannot produce righteousness. So what hope is there for righteousness in the world today? Only one, and that is that some people will hunger for righteousness and pursue it, not because of regulation but because they actually want it.

Think of the difference it would make in any business or profession if people truly hungered after righteousness. Imagine if instead of asking, "What's in it for me?" people would begin to ask, "What would honor God and be good for others, as well as for me?" To those people who hunger and thirst for righteousness, Jesus says, "You are the salt of the earth. . . . You are the light of the world" (Matt. 5:13–14). People who hunger for righteousness are blessed, and they will also be a blessing to all who are around them.

What do you know of this hunger in your life? Is righteousness what you long for, or are you focused on something else? Look around a Christian bookstore and you will find evidence that many who profess to be Christians are looking for happy families, growing churches, and personal fulfillment. We long to be blessed, but Jesus does not say that we are *righteous* if we hunger and thirst to be *blessed*. He says we are *blessed* if we hunger and thirst to be *righteous*.

THE PARADOX OF SATISFACTION

*"Blessed are those who hunger and thirst
for righteousness,* for they shall be satisfied."
(Matthew 5:6, emphasis added)

Choose the wrong thirsts and you will never be satisfied. If money grabs your heart, you will never have enough. Desire for money is insatiable, and the same is true for other sins of the flesh. If lust takes control, your heart will always burn; where pride takes root, no affirmation will ever be enough for you; and where sloth sets in, you will always feel that you need more time for rest. Hell is a place of unending hungers and thirsts, where the soul is always being destroyed because it can never be fulfilled. There is never a path from sin to satisfaction.

Every person is on a quest for satisfaction. What do you think will satisfy you? And where do you think you will find it? Your answer to these two questions matters because whatever you think will satisfy you will become the consuming passion of your life. If you think that satisfaction is found in achievement, then achievement will be the goal of your life. If you feel that satisfaction will be found in relationships or in sports and leisure, these will become your aims and your goals. Jesus tells us that there is one desire, and only one, that will be fully satisfied: "Blessed are those who hunger and thirst *for righteousness,* for they shall be satisfied."

The paradox in the fourth beatitude is that our Lord speaks about hungering and being satisfied at the same time. We experience these as alternatives; when you are hungry you are not satisfied, and when you are satisfied you are no longer hungry. But Christ speaks of a deep hunger and a profound satisfaction that grow together in the same human heart.

A. W. Pink asked, "Can one who has been brought into vital union with Him who is the Bread of Life . . . be found still hungering and thirsting?" His answer is unequivocal: "Yes, such is the experience of the renewed heart."[7] Martyn Lloyd-Jones concurs: "The Christian is one who at one and the same time is hungering and thirsting, and yet he is filled. And the more he is filled, the more he hungers and thirsts. That is the blessedness of the Christian life. It goes on."[8]

Godly men and women have found joy in this mystery through the ages. Bernard of Clairvaux, writing in the twelfth century, penned these beautiful words that capture the paradox of hungering and being satisfied at the same time:

> We taste Thee, O Thou living bread
> And long to feast upon Thee still.
> We drink of Thee, the Fountainhead
> And Thirst our souls from Thee to fill.[9]

DIET, APPETITE, AND TIME

So what can you do to cultivate a greater hunger and thirst for righteousness? How would you go about making yourself hungry?

Some time ago, when I was preaching on this fourth beatitude, a lady in our congregation made a comment that I have found profoundly helpful. "Hunger is natural," she said, "but appetite can be cultivated." That's a useful distinction. Hunger for righteousness arises from within, and it is formed by the Holy Spirit in the soul of every person who has been born again, but appetite can and should be cultivated. When Paul says, "Train yourself for godliness" (1 Tim. 4:7), he clearly communicates that there are some things we can do that will help us move forward in a life that is pleasing to God.

103

A colleague of mine, who survived a major heart attack, told me his ordeal was "like an elephant sitting on my chest." In the kindness of God he has made a good recovery, and part of that recovery has involved a complete change of diet. When I asked him what he liked to eat before the heart attack, he said, "Burgers, fries, pizza, and ice cream." So there was no surprise when, after the heart attack, the doctor told my friend that he needed a complete change of diet. On hearing the new menu—"Low fat, low sodium, vegetables, fish, chicken (grilled, not fried), and some rice"—my friend had said, "This is going to be absolute torture!"

So I asked him how the change of diet had gone. "At first it all seemed bland and tasteless," he said, "but after a while I thought, *This is not so bad.* I felt better, and I had more energy." He told me that he didn't miss the burgers as much as he had thought, and when he had a craving for pizza or fries, he thought about the elephant sitting on his chest. "Burgers and fries still smell good," he said, "but over a period of about two months, my appetite changed."

Appetite can be cultivated. Think about what happened to my friend: a change of diet led to a change of appetite. Diet shapes appetite over time.

The congregation that I serve has a healthy appetite for the Word of God. People who visit our church are often struck by this, and wonder where that came from. The answer is simple. The appetite came from the diet, and it has been cultivated over time. For more than sixty years, this congregation has been feeding on the Word of God, and the diet has shaped the appetite.

This principle holds true whatever the diet happens to be: Feed a congregation entertainment, and you will create an appetite for entertainment. Feed a congregation pop psychology, and they will have a hunger and thirst for more. This principle is really important in choosing the church where you will worship, serve, and be fed. What is the diet? I have often found myself mystified over the incongruity of people who care deeply about what they feed to their bodies, but seem quite happy to keep loading junk food into their souls. Diet shapes appetite over time, so get yourself to a church where the diet will cultivate a hunger and thirst for God and His righteousness, rather than for yourself and your fulfillment.

FIVE STRATEGIES FOR CULTIVATING A GODLY APPETITE

Just as one can change a diet and still cultivate an appetite over time, so we can begin to change deeply engrained habits and cultivate a godly appetite. Here are five strategies for doing so.

1. Gain momentum from the first three beatitudes.

By this stage in our journey, you might have guessed that this would be the first point, so I will deal with it briefly. But it is too important to miss!

The Beatitudes are progressive. Each beatitude assumes the ones that have gone before. You can't just hunger and thirst for righteousness; you have to start from the beginning. This does not mean you have to spend a week being poor in spirit and a month mourning over your sins before you can move on. The momentum of realizing your poverty before God, seeing your own sins, and submitting yourself to the will of God may happen at the same time. The point is simply that if progress is to be made, none of these can be missing.

You can't start at the fourth beatitude and decide that you want to have a great hunger for holiness. But here's the encouragement: as you become poor in spirit, mourn your sins, and submit your life to the will of God, you *will* find that a true hunger for righteousness springs from these roots.

2. Practice fasting from legitimate pleasures.

One sure way to spoil your appetite is to snack between meals. If you snack on chips throughout the afternoon, you won't have much appetite for dinner in the evening. So restrict what spoils your appetite. Don't snack between meals.

The point here is not that there is something wicked or sinful about a bag of chips, but eating at the wrong time and in the wrong amount will spoil your appetite. Now let's apply that obvious principle from the world of the body to the world of the soul: legitimate pleasures at the wrong time and in the wrong amount will spoil your appetite for righteousness. They will make you dull and sluggish in following after Christ.

GAINING MOMENTUM / Five Strategies for Cultivating a Godly Appetite

1. *Gain momentum from the first three beatitudes.* Don't try to start at the fourth beatitude and decide that you want to have a great hunger for holiness. Remember, the Beatitudes are progressive. As you become poor in spirit, mourn your sins, and submit your life to the will of God, you *will* find that a true hunger for righteousness springs from these roots.

2. *Practice fasting from legitimate pleasures.* Legitimate pleasures at the wrong time and in the wrong amount will spoil your appetite for righteousness. They will make you dull and sluggish in following after Christ. One way to keep the legitimate pleasures of life, like sports, travel, and hobbies, in their proper place is to fast periodically from such pleasures, a means of heightening self-control. Wean yourself off the unhealthy appetites that are shaping (or even dominating) your life, and strengthen your hunger and thirst for Christ.

3. *Make yourself vulnerable to the needs of others.* Extend yourself in serving others and you will find that your hunger and thirst for righteousness will increase. Combine this

Are the legitimate pleasures of your life holding you back from becoming all that Christ calls you to be? Is your appetite for God being diminished by your hunger and thirst for other things? What are these things? You like to work out? You like to sleep? You like to watch sports or movies? Play golf? There's nothing wrong with any of these, but diet shapes appetite over time. What you consume becomes what you desire.

So how can you keep the legitimate pleasures of life, like sports, travel, and hobbies, in their proper place? One answer is by periodically fasting from legitimate pleasures. Fasting is a means of heightening self-control. It is a special gift that can be used to help you master something that otherwise might master you.

If your diet has created an appetite that you now see is holding you

strategy together with the previous one: fast from some legitimate pleasure, at least for a time, and use the time, energy, and resources you gain from this to make yourself vulnerable to the needs of others.

4. *Use your blessings and troubles as incentives to feed on Christ.* The best and the worst things that happen in your life can both be used to stimulate your hunger and thirst for God. Whatever the situation, whether trouble or persecution or blessing, allow it to increase your hunger for righteousness. We are to use the different circumstances of our lives to motivate a more vigorous pursuit of righteousness. Whatever happens, use the situation to strengthen a godly appetite.

5. *Trust Christ especially for your sanctification.* Christians believe they can trust Christ to forgive their sins and get them to heaven. Yet some forget that He also came to deliver men and women from all that holds them back from the pursuit of a righteous and godly life. John the apostle says our hope of being with Jesus one day can move us toward a godly life now (see 1 John 3:2–3). Change begins when you say, "In Christ there is hope for me to be a better person."

back from a more useful life, implement a fast. Take a month without TV or computer games, or without golf, or six months without buying new clothes, or without leisure travel. Drop a sport for a semester. You will be surprised at the freedom this can bring you.

Alexander Maclaren says, "A man who lets all his longings go unchecked and untamed after earthly good has none left towards heaven."[10] Using a helpful picture, he points out that if a river divides into many channels there will be little or no force in its current. In the same way, if we dissipate our desires into the many legitimate pleasures and interests we can pursue in this world, we fritter them away, and have no strength of desire left to hunger and thirst after God.

Fasting has the effect of cleansing the body, and the same thing can happen in your soul by choosing to deny yourself a legitimate pleasure for a season. Fasting is a great way to bring appetites that have become too strong back under control. Some Christians do this in the period leading up to Easter by "giving something up for Lent." Why wait for Lent? Wean yourself off the unhealthy appetites that are shaping your life, and strengthen your hunger and thirst for Christ.

3. Make yourself vulnerable to the needs of others.

How do you work up a good appetite? By getting some good exercise. Go for a brisk walk or a run, and when you come back, you find yourself ready for a good meal.

The same principle holds true when it comes to nourishing your soul. Extend yourself in serving others and you will find that your hunger and thirst for righteousness will increase. I have been moved by the initiatives many in our church have taken to move in this direction. One of our small groups volunteered to staff a homeless shelter and as a result of that experience, they committed to doing this on a regular basis. A number from our congregation are regularly visiting folks in prison. Others give themselves to visiting the sick or to advocating for those who are persecuted for their faith.

Put this strategy together with the previous one: fast from some legitimate pleasure, at least for a time, and use the time, energy, and resources you gain from this to make yourself vulnerable to the needs of others.

4. Use your blessings and troubles as incentives to feed on Christ.

Once again, I have been greatly helped here by Thomas Watson, the pithy Puritan who was blessed with so many remarkable insights. Writing on how we can stimulate a spiritual appetite, he noted two things that make us ready to eat a hearty meal. The first was exercise. That seems pretty obvious to me, but his second answer took me by surprise: "There are two things that provoke appetite. 1. Exercise. 2. Sauce!"

Watson is right. Sauce makes food more attractive, and God can use the sweet sauce of our blessings, the sharp sauce of our troubles, and the hot sauce of our persecutions to increase our hunger for righteousness. You may not have thought of your blessings, troubles, and persecutions as sauce before, but I think Watson was onto something important here. We are to use the different circumstances of our lives as incentives to motivate a more vigorous pursuit of righteousness. The best and the worst things that happen in your life can both be used to stimulate your hunger and thirst for God.

When blessing comes, you can learn to say, "God is so good; I want to know more of Him." When trouble or persecution comes, you can learn to say, "My flesh and my heart may fail, but God is the strength of my heart and my portion forever" (Ps. 73:26). Whatever happens, use it to strengthen a godly appetite.

5. Trust Christ especially for your sanctification.

Some Christians feel they can trust Christ to forgive their sins and get them to heaven, but when it comes to growing in godliness and becoming more like Christ, they feel completely hopeless.

But think about this: Christ came to save people from their sins (Matt. 1:21). His work was not limited to dealing with the guilt of your sins or even to the consequences of your sins. He came to deliver you from all that holds you back from the pursuit of a righteous and godly life. If you can trust Jesus Christ for forgiveness and for entrance into heaven, why is it so difficult for you to trust Him for progress in your pursuit of righteousness?

Christ gives you this great promise: your hunger and thirst for righteousness will be satisfied. When God's people are before His throne, "they shall *hunger* no more, neither *thirst* anymore. . . . For the Lamb in the midst of the throne will be their shepherd, and he will guide them to springs of living water" (Rev. 7:16–17, emphasis added).

When you see Christ, you will be like Him, and when you know that one day you will be fully like Christ, you will purify yourself, even as Christ is pure (1 John 3:2–3). If you can trust Christ to complete His redeeming work in you then, why should you not trust Him to advance His redeeming work in you now? Change begins when you say, "In Christ there is hope for me to be a better person. Through Him I can pursue a righteous life."

A. W. Tozer penned a prayer that is a heart-cry for holiness, the response of a heart with a deep longing for God.

O God, I have tasted Your goodness, and it has both satisfied me and made me thirsty for more. I am painfully conscious of my need of further grace. I am ashamed of my lack of desire.

O God, the Triune God, I want to want You. I long to be filled with longing; I thirst to be made more thirsty still.

Show me Your glory, I pray that I may know You indeed. Begin in mercy a new work of love within me. Say to my soul "Rise up my love and come away." Then give me the grace to rise and follow You, up from this misty lowland where I have wandered so long.

In Jesus' Name, Amen.[11]

"Blessed are the merciful, for they shall receive mercy."

MATTHEW 5:7

5

I CARE
ABOUT OTHERS

THE JOY OF COMPLETE FORGIVENESS

Most people want to forgive, but some don't know how to get there. If a great wrong has been done to you, you may feel that forgiveness is impossible. However desirable forgiveness might be, it towers over you like a mountain that you cannot climb.

In this chapter, we will explore how you can pursue mercy and forgiveness. These twin virtues belong together, and it is important to understand the relationship between them: mercy is broader than forgiveness, but forgiveness goes further than mercy.

The story of the good Samaritan shows why mercy is broader than forgiveness. The Samaritan showed mercy to a man who was lying in the road (Luke 10:37). The wounded man had not wronged the Samaritan in any way. Lying in the road, he did not need forgiveness but he did need mercy, which the Samaritan gave by binding up his wounds and then taking him to a place of safety where he could recover.

You will often have the opportunity of showing mercy in situations where no wrong has been done to you and where there is nothing for you to forgive.

Mercy is broader than forgiveness, but forgiveness goes further than mercy. Suppose someone wrongs you. To be merciful means that you have compassion on that person, and rather than return harm, you seek to do him good. Mercy chooses not to repay evil for evil, but rather, to "overcome evil with good" (Rom. 12:21). But forgiveness goes further because it involves restoring a relationship. So mercy is like a stepping-stone to forgiveness. Pursue mercy and you will get to forgiveness.

Mercy is the central theme of the story of the good Samaritan. A man on a journey is attacked, robbed, beaten, and left for dead. A traveler comes along, sees the need, but passes by on the other side. Later, another traveler comes to the same spot and also passes by.

Then Jesus says, "But a Samaritan, as he journeyed, came to where he was, and when he saw him, he had compassion. He went to him and bound up his wounds, pouring on oil and wine" (Luke 10:33–34). At the end of the story Jesus asks: "Which of these three . . . proved to be a neighbor to the man who fell among the robbers?" Answer: "The one who showed him mercy" (vv. 36–37).

This is a parable about *mercy* and, according to Jesus, mercy has two parts: First, there is a tenderness of heart: "When he saw him, he had compassion." Second, there is the action that arises from a compassionate heart: "He went to him and bound up his wounds, pouring on oil and wine" (vv. 33–34).

GOD'S CHARACTER AND OUR CALLING

When God appeared to Moses at Sinai, He revealed Himself in a fourfold description that is repeated no less than seven times in the

Old Testament:[1] "The Lord, the Lord, a God merciful and gracious, slow to anger, and abounding in steadfast love" (Ex. 34:6).

Here is what redeemed people most need to know about God. He is gracious, merciful, slow to anger, and abounding in love. Mercy is at the heart of what God tells us about Himself, and mercy means that God has a tender heart, and that out of compassion He acts for your good.

The rest of the Bible takes up this marvelous theme. Not only is God merciful, He is "rich is mercy" (Eph. 2:4). His mercy never changes, and this is why David is able to say, "Surely goodness and mercy shall follow me all the days of my life" (Ps. 23:6). It is because of God's mercy that we are saved (Titus 3:5), and when Paul describes God's saving intervention in his life, he says, "I received mercy" (1 Tim. 1:13).

The book of Hebrews focuses on the *mercy of Christ*. "He had to be made like his brothers in every respect, so that he might become a *merciful* and faithful high priest" (Heb. 2:17, emphasis added). In Jesus Christ God says to His people, "I will be merciful toward their iniquities, and I will remember their sins no more" (8:12). When you know that Jesus is your *merciful* High Priest, you will feel both the freedom and the desire to come to Him (4:16).

CHRIST'S MERCY TO PETER AND THOMAS

The mercy of Jesus is on display throughout the Gospels. Think about His mercy to Peter: our Lord warned His disciple, "The rooster will not crow till you have denied me three times" (John 13:38). Peter's denial of Jesus was the kind of failure that would leave him wondering, "How in the world did I end up doing that?" But Christ prayed for Peter that his faith would not fail (Luke 22:31) and although Peter failed in his testimony, the reality of his faith was shown by the fact that he could not live with his denial of Jesus. Peter's faith produced repentance. After Jesus' resurrection, when He showed Himself to four of His disciples on the shore of the Sea of Galilee, He asked Peter, "Do you love me?" Peter answered, "Lord, you know that I love you." And Christ said to him, "Feed my sheep" (John 21:15–17). Mercy means that your failure need never have the last word.

Earlier Jesus had demonstrated His mercy to Thomas, a man in spiritual leadership whose own faith was not in good shape. The unanswered questions were piling up for him, and in his heart he must have felt that he was slipping away. He told the inner circle of disciples, "Unless I see in his hands the mark of the nails . . . I will never believe." But Christ never lets His children go. The Savior appeared to Thomas: "Put your finger here, and see my hands. . . . Do not disbelieve, but believe" (John 20:25, 27). Mercy means that your doubts and questions need never have the last word.

The whole point of the Christian life is that the character of Jesus be reproduced in the lives of His people, and that means a community of brothers and sisters who have compassionate hearts and act for the good of others. This is central to our calling. What God requires of us is "to act justly and *to love mercy* and to walk humbly with your God" (Mic. 6:8 NIV, emphasis added). That is why, to some leaders who misunderstood what God requires of us, Jesus said, "Go and learn what this means, 'I desire mercy, and not sacrifice'" (Matt. 9:13).

Learn to show mercy. You will make a difference in your business, your church, and your family circle. Think of the difference that a teacher who is merciful can make in a school. One teacher with a tender heart who acts for the good of the children, the staff, and those in the administration will make that difference at a point where it is needed and in a way that honors your Lord.

OPPORTUNITIES FOR SHOWING MERCY

So let's think about seven opportunities for showing mercy. The first is pretty obvious: when you cross paths with someone who has material need.

That was the case with the Good Samaritan who responded to the needs of the man in the road, beaten and bleeding. Sinclair Ferguson said it well: "Mercy is getting down on your hands and knees and doing something to restore dignity to someone whose life has been broken by sin."[2] He pointed out that the Samaritan did not deal with the cause of the man's need by chasing the robbers. Nor did the Samaritan complain about the failure of society to meet the man's need. Instead, he addressed the immediate need that was set before him and did what he could to bring relief. God will bring people in material need across your path, and when He does, you have an opportunity to reflect His likeness by showing mercy.

A second opportunity for showing mercy comes when you encounter a fellow Christian who is struggling in his or her walk with God. When Jude says, "Have mercy on those who doubt" (Jude 22), he reminds us that when a brother or sister in Christ is plagued with unanswered questions, their greatest need is the kindness and compassion of a believing friend who will come alongside and strengthen them in their faith.

I once heard Pastor Warren Wiersbe[3] say that if he could go back and do one thing differently he would do more to encourage God's people. The statement was striking to me because Warren is one of the most encouraging people I have ever met. If he wished he had done more to encourage others, how much more should I?

People who doubt will not be helped by a harsh and demanding ministry. Christ does not break "a bruised reed" (Isa. 42:3). David tells us that it was God's *gentleness* that made him great (Ps. 18:35). Your usefulness to Christ will increase as you become more tender toward others and sensitive to the loads they bear.

A third opportunity for showing mercy comes when someone fails in a way that might bring them shame and embarrassment. "Love covers a multitude of sins," the apostle Peter writes (1 Peter 4:8), and a merciful person will look for ways to spare the blushes of the one who has failed.

Clearly, there are some things that should not be covered over. Peter speaks about sins, not crimes, and there is an important difference. But there are many sins that a merciful person can gladly and rightly hide from view. Spurgeon says, "I recommend you, brothers and sisters, always to have one blind eye and one deaf ear." Notice he speaks about one eye and one ear! Christ calls us to be "as wise as serpents" as well as harmless like doves, and going through life with both ears closed would be a recipe for disaster! But Spurgeon speaks with godly wisdom when he says, "My blind eye is the best eye that I have, and my deaf ear is the best ear I have."[4]

A hard heart always makes a big deal of another person's failure, but a merciful heart will often lead you to turn a blind eye and a deaf ear. God does not treat us as our sins deserve or repay us according to our iniquities. He is merciful, and love covers over a multitude of sins.

A fourth opportunity for showing mercy is in how we treat a juicy piece of gossip. Remember, Satan is called the father of lies. He is always manufacturing rumors that would make a person think less of their brothers or sisters in Christ, and some Christians seem to be adept at helping him!

Thomas Watson points out that it is as bad to believe a lie as it is to tell one, and that it is as bad to repeat a lie as it is to invent one. I have found that convicting. We live in a culture where verdicts are often announced before evidence is properly heard, and we need to guard against the churlish spirit that is quick to believe the worst and slow to think the best of others. When that habit takes root, it is easy to slide into making more of other people's failings than you do of their strengths and virtues. But mercy goes the other way and makes more of a person's virtues than of their failings.

A merciful person will close his or her ears to anything that would diminish their view of someone else, unless compelled to do otherwise. Watson said, "A man's name is worth more than his goods, and . . . he that takes away the good name of another sins more than if he had taken the corn out of his field or the goods out of his shop. . . . Better take away a man's life than his name. It is an irreparable injury."[5]

A fifth way to show mercy is by having reasonable expectations. Other Christians will, by their fragile nature, disappoint us and let us down, just as we will often disappoint others and fail them. God remembers that I am dust and I must remember this in relation to others. I must not set unreasonable expectations of my spouse, my children, or others who work with me. I must learn not to be surprised by discouragements and disappointments. I must get beyond thinking that a person will be a consistent paragon of virtue simply because he or she is a Christian. If we think more about the heavy burdens others may carry and the strong temptations they may face, we will grow in mercy. Always remember that if you were carrying your brother's burden or facing your sister's temptation, you might struggle and fail more than they do.

A sixth opportunity to show mercy comes when someone hurts or wrongs you. Joseph's brothers wronged him terribly, but God blessed him, and he became the prime minister of Egypt. When the brothers needed food, they came to Egypt and Joseph had them in his power. God orchestrated events in Joseph's life so that he would have the opportunity to get even—or to forgive. Joseph chose to forgive his brothers. That's what mercy does. If you have been wounded by another person, don't be surprised if, at some point, God puts you in a position where you have the opportunity to pay them back. If that happens, what you do at that moment will reveal a great deal about you.

A seventh way to show mercy relates to presenting the gospel to someone who is not yet a believer in Christ. Merciful people often speak to Christ about the lost and they often speak to the lost about Christ. Jude exhorts us to "save others by snatching them out of the fire; to others show *mercy* with fear" (Jude 23, emphasis added). Augustine said, "If I weep for the body from which the soul is departed, how should I not weep for the soul from which God is departed?"[6] A tender heart that cares and acts for the good of others will care deeply about people without Christ, and will act by sharing the gospel with them.

Put these seven situations together and you will see that there are multiple opportunities for practicing mercy. People facing material needs, spiritual struggles, and embarrassing failures all need the gift of mercy. God calls you to mercy when you hear slanderous gossip, have high expectations, or suffer personal injury. Most of all, as someone who is trusted with the gospel in a world of lost people, you can practice mercy by speaking of the Savior who delivers all who put their trust in Him.

We began this chapter by saying that most people want to forgive, but some don't know how to get there. We have seen that mercy is a stepping-stone to forgiveness. Pursuing mercy will get you to a place where you are ready and able to forgive, and it is to this theme of forgiveness that we now turn.

HOW AND WHEN GOD FORGIVES

Think with me for a moment about how and when God forgives. God forgives (1) where a wrong has been done, (2) when repentance begins, and (3) because atonement has been made.

God forgives where a wrong has been done.

If I were to say to you, "I forgive you," you might reasonably say, "Whatever for? I haven't wronged you, so what is there for you to forgive?" Forgiveness is only appropriate and it is only meaningful when a wrong has been done. As Lewis Smedes puts it, "Forgiveness always comes with blame attached."[7]

When God forgives us, it means that we have wronged Him. Every sin in your life and mine is a personal offense against God. Saul of Tarsus was on a campaign in which he persecuted Christians, but when Christ appeared to him on the Damascus road, He said, "Saul, Saul, why do you persecute *Me*?" The violence that Saul perpetrated was against Christians, but the sin that he committed was against Christ.

David captured the same truth in Psalm 51. Confessing his sin of adultery, he said to God, "Against you, you only, have I sinned" (v. 4). Clearly there was a profound sense in which he had wronged the woman he had slept with, he had wronged her husband, and he had wronged his own wife. But David knew that all of his sins were offenses against God, and that even if he were to be forgiven by all of the people he had wronged, God was the One to whom he must ultimately give account. God was the one from whom he most needed to receive forgiveness.

God forgives where a wrong has been done, when repentance begins.

The story of the prodigal son makes this wonderfully clear. The son leaves home in rebellion, but when he comes to his senses he has a change of heart, and begins the long journey home. He doesn't expect much but hopes that his father might take him on as a hired servant.

The father sees the son from a distance and rather than wait, he runs out to meet him. This pictures the wonderful truth that God rushes out to meet His prodigal children and to embrace us in His loving forgiveness at the first sign of our repentance.

Repenting is a process that every believer begins, but none of us completes in this life. Our repentance toward God is at best a small part of what it should be. Thank God, He forgives us when our repentance begins, not when it is complete. If it were not for this, no one would ever be forgiven.

There is something important to be learned here in regard to our forgiving and being reconciled to others. When someone who has wronged you begins to repent, move toward the person with love and forgiveness. Remember that the father did not sit in the house waiting with folded arms until the son trudged every last step of the way home. At the first sign of the son's return, he ran toward him with love and forgiveness. So don't wait until every aspect of an offense has been owned. Don't insist on a complete understanding of all that has been involved. You don't have a full understanding of the extent of your sins against God, but He chose to forgive you, not at the end, but at the beginning of your repentance.

God forgives when repentance *begins,* but it is also true that His forgiveness is tied to the beginning of *repentance.* The Bible never suggests there is forgiveness without repentance. To people who rejected Him, Jesus said, "I am going away, and you will seek me, and you will die in your sin" (John 8:21).

The principle of forgiveness being given when repentance begins is important when we come to the difficult question of forgiving a person who isn't even sorry for what they have done. What is your responsibility in a situation when a person who has wronged you shows no awareness of what he or she has done, takes no responsibility for it, and for that reason may well commit the same sin against you or against someone else again in the future?

I think it is important to note that God does *not* forgive unrepentant sinners. The Bible tells us that He loves them, and this is what God calls us to do: "Love your enemies and pray for those who persecute you" (Matt. 5:44). Notice, God does not say, "Forgive your enemies." He says, "Love them, pray for them," because that is what God Himself does. So when someone wrongs you and takes no responsibility for their actions, your calling is to *have compassion toward them and to pray for them.*

One important difference between love and forgiveness is that love can be one-sided. It is possible to love a person who does not love you back. Loving your enemy will always be one-sided. As long as a person is your enemy, they will not love you back, and if your love should win them, they would no longer be your enemy. Love can be one-directional but forgiveness is relational. Two parties are involved, one forgiving and the other being forgiven and in this transaction, a relationship is restored.

I've heard wise and respected Christian teachers talk about forgiving an unrepentant person, but that involves asking you to do something that God Himself never does, and it undermines the sacred truth that God's forgiveness always leads to a restored relationship.

You may ask, "Did Jesus not forgive the soldiers who nailed Him to the cross?" Yes, but Jesus did not say to the unrepentant soldiers, "I forgive you." He turned to heaven and prayed that His Father would forgive. The distinction is important.

Forgiveness involves the reconciling of two people—one who repents and the other who forgives—and I believe that it is a mistake to tell people that they must forgive where there is no repentance. It is more faithful to Scripture to say that we must love an unrepentant person, have compassion on them, and pray for them. If we do this, we will be ready to release forgiveness wherever and whenever it will be received.

God forgives because atonement has been made.

God forgives where a wrong has been done, when repentance begins, because atonement has been made. Think of how extraordinarily difficult it is for God to forgive. When God was creating the world, all He had to do was speak it into existence: "'Let there be light,' and there was light" (Gen. 1:3). But when it came to forgiveness, He could not simply say, "Let them be forgiven." It was harder than that—much harder.

It took God Himself entering our world, taking on human flesh, living a perfect life, shedding His own blood, and laying down His life on the cross.

When someone says, "I know that God forgives me, but I can't forgive myself," I want to ask, "Are you saying that it is easier for God to forgive you than it is for you to forgive yourself?" The root problem here is pride. You are putting yourself above God. You are saying, "The blood of Christ may be good enough for God, but it is not good enough for me."

So here's how you forgive yourself for the things that bring you guilt and shame today: say to yourself, "If the blood of Christ is good enough to satisfy the Father in relation to my sin, why should it not be good enough to satisfy me?"

God forgives where a wrong has been done, when repentance begins, because atonement has been made. Having looked at these foundations, we are ready to answer our central question, "How can I get to the place of being ready to forgive others, as God in His great mercy has forgiven me?"

SIX STRIDES TOWARD FORGIVENESS

Imagine standing next to a hurdle on a race track. You are right up against it, and you can't jump over it from a standing position. You have to back up and take a run at the hurdle.

Think about that picture in relation to your spiritual life. It is easy to get focused on one sin or problem that you want to overcome. *How do I get over my fear? How can I prevail over this lust?* There you are, standing right next to the hurdle, and you can't move forward from that position. You have to begin further back. You have to take a run at it and get some momentum.

I've found that in trying to help a person who is struggling with one particular battle, it is important to look not only at the problem, but also at their general spiritual health. Is this person regularly engaged in worship? Do they pray? Is there a pattern of regularly feeding on the Word of God? Is this person part of a small group where they are able to walk with and encourage others? Cultivating your general spiritual health will enable you to take a run at the hurdle and to overcome the particular battle that has become so troublesome for you.

So let's apply this to the challenge of forgiving a wrong that has been done to you. Standing next to it, you have felt that you were up against a barrier you could never get over, but now you are backing up to take a run at it. How do you get over that hurdle? Everything you need for the run-up is gathered together in the final verses of Ephesians 4, where Paul writes:

> Do not grieve the Holy Spirit of God, by whom you were sealed for the day of redemption. Let all bitterness and wrath and anger and clamor and slander be put away from you, along with all malice. Be kind to one another, tenderhearted, forgiving one another, as God in Christ forgave you. (vv. 30–32)

Six strides that will get you to forgiveness are presented in these verses:

1. Remember that the Holy Spirit lives in you.

. . . the Holy Spirit of God, by whom you were sealed. (v. 30)

You may have experienced hurts and wounds that are extremely hard to forgive, hurts that I know nothing about, hurts that are deeper than anything I've ever experienced, but here's what you need to know: no one has had more to forgive than God. Every sin you have ever committed is a sin against Him—and that is true not only of your sins, but of every sin of every believer who has ever lived.

But God has forgiven *all* of these sins, and His Spirit now lives in you through His Son. Forgiveness may be beyond your capacity, if it depended on you alone, but you can gain momentum in your run at forgiveness with the great truth that the Spirit of God is at work in you.

2. Don't dwell on the injury.

Let all bitterness and wrath and anger . . . be put away from you. (v. 31)

Bitterness, wrath, and anger all come from nursing a grievance. Someone has wronged you, and your mind keeps rehearsing it over and over again. You keep thinking about it—how wrong it was, how hurtful it was. But every time you think about it, you are stoking a fire in your soul.

Bitterness and anger are fires that need to be fed, so stop feeding them! When your mind goes back to that stuff, say to yourself, "There are better things to fill my mind with than this." With the help of the Holy Spirit, set your mind on things that are true, honorable, just, pure, lovely, commendable, and excellent. Fill your mind with things that are

GAINING MOMENTUM / Six Strides toward Forgiveness

1. *Remember that the Holy Spirit lives in you.* The Holy Spirit who convicts you to believe (John 16:7–8) now lives in you through God's Son. Forgiveness may be beyond your capacity, if it depended on you alone, but you can gain momentum in your run at forgiveness with the great truth that the Spirit of God is at work in you.

2. *Don't dwell on the injury.* When someone has wronged you, your mind begins to rehearse that wrong over and over. Bitterness, wrath, and anger all come from nursing a grievance. When your mind begins to rehearse once more, ask the Holy Spirit to set your mind on things that are true, honorable, just, pure, lovely, commendable, and excellent—those things that are "worthy of praise" (Phil. 4:8).

3. *Don't fight and quarrel.* If you're going to take a run at the hurdle of forgiveness, you have to get clamor, slander, and malice out of the way (Eph. 4:31; 2 Tim. 2:24). Avoid dwelling on the pain of past injuries, which will get in the way of forgiveness and steal your momentum.

"worthy of praise," and you will gather speed as you move toward the hurdle of forgiveness (Phil. 4:8).

3. Don't fight and quarrel.

Let . . . clamor and slander be put away from you, along with all malice. (v. 31)

When a relationship is in trouble, fighting over who did what or who said what can make it worse. The Scriptures warn, "The Lord's servant must not be quarrelsome" (2 Tim. 2:24). Quarreling stokes the fires of bitterness and anger, putting you further from the forgiveness you're trying to cultivate.

Clamor and slander involve dredging up and passing on the faults and failings of another person. So to "put away" clamor and slander

4. *Have compassion toward the one who has hurt you.* If someone has wronged you but still has no idea of what she has done, show her compassion. If he has not taken ownership of his action, demonstrate pity. Why? Jesus had compassion toward the crowds because they were "like sheep without a shepherd" (Matt. 9:36). They didn't even know they were lost, and the person who has sinned against you may be just like that. God can use your wounds to increase your compassion.

5. *Realize that you will need the forgiveness of others.* Forgiveness will inevitably travel in both directions. There will be things you need to forgive in others, and you can be certain that there will be things others need to forgive in you. Realizing your own need of continuing forgiveness will help you to take another stride toward the hurdle of forgiving others.

6. *Savor your forgiveness in Christ.* God's forgiveness is both the model and the motive of our forgiving. That is why the apostle draws our attention to *the way* in which we have been forgiven by God. He did it gladly, freely, and fully. Your forgiveness is undeserved. Let this priceless gift of God that you have received move your heart to forgive others as God in Christ forgave you.

means that I am not to vent about another person or to bad-mouth them to others. Malice is the desire that a person who has hurt you will get what they deserve. So "putting away" malice means that I am not to comfort myself by savoring the thought of what they deserve.

Dwelling on the pain of past injuries will get in the way of forgiveness and steal your momentum. If you're going to take a run at the hurdle of forgiveness, you have to get clamor, slander, and malice out of the way.

4. Have compassion toward the one who has hurt you.

Be kind to one another, tender-hearted . . . (v. 32)

Compassion is especially important when a person who has wronged you has no idea of what he or she has done. She is completely unrepentant. He has not taken ownership. She has no sense of responsibility. He is blind to what he is doing and completely unaware of the pain that he is causing.

Well, if this person is blind, you should have pity. When you see a person on the street who's completely blind, do you want to run up and kick their cane away? No! You have compassion. When Jesus saw the crowds, He had compassion on them because they were "like sheep without a shepherd" (Matt. 9:36). They didn't even know they were lost, and the person who has sinned against you may be just like that.

Jesus became the merciful, tenderhearted High Priest He is through what He suffered (Heb. 2:17). Suffering often produces hardness of heart but it does not have to. God can use your wounds to increase your compassion, and being tenderhearted will move you even closer to the hurdle of forgiveness.

5. Realize that you will need the forgiveness of others.

Forgiving one another . . . (v. 32)

God does not say here, "Forgive the one who has hurt you," as if the forgiveness were only moving in one direction. He says, "Forgive one another," because forgiveness will inevitably travel in both directions.

There will be things you need to forgive in others, and you can be absolutely certain that there will be things others need to forgive in you.

No matter how much you progress in your Christian life, you will always be in the position of saying, "Lord, have mercy on me," and realizing your own need of continuing forgiveness will help you to take another stride toward the hurdle of forgiving others.

6. Savor your forgiveness in Christ.

Forgiving one another, as God in Christ forgave you. (v. 32)

God's forgiveness is both the model and the motive of our forgiving. That is why the apostle draws our attention to *the way* in which we have been forgiven by God.

Think about how God has forgiven you in Christ. He did it gladly, freely, and fully. Your forgiveness is undeserved, it is irreversible, and it is eternal. God has forgiven you in love and mercy, out of an agony of heart, shrouded in darkness at Calvary, and you will never fully understand that pain, even to all eternity.

Savor your forgiveness in Christ. Appreciate it. Enjoy it. Let this priceless gift of God that you have received move your heart to worship, wonder, love, and praise, and your heart will be ready to forgive others as God in Christ forgave you.

GOING OVER THE HURDLE

Practice these six strides, and your seventh stride will take you over the hurdle of forgiveness. If you are mindful of the Holy Spirit in your life, you will have the confidence to forgive. If you resist the temptation to fight, quarrel, and dwell on your injuries, your way to forgiveness will be clear. If you have compassion on those who hurt you and see your need for mercy, you will be ready to forgive. And if you savor your forgiveness in Christ, you will want to extend the same forgiveness to others. These practices really do work, and if you pursue them, you will be able to forgive.

Even when a person has hurt you badly, and is completely unaware of what he or she has done, if you practice these six strides, you will be ready at any moment to forgive. Forgiveness will be in your heart and you will be ready to place it in the hands of the one who has wronged you, whenever he or she is ready to receive the gift.

"Blessed are the pure in heart, for they shall see God."

MATTHEW 5:8

6

I GO AFTER
ONE THING

THE FOCUS OF SINGLE-MINDEDNESS

When I read about being pure in heart, my first reaction is, "That doesn't sound like me," and I suspect that may be your reaction as well. It's easy to relate to Jesus when He says, "Blessed are the poor in spirit," and "Blessed are those who mourn." But when Jesus says, "Blessed are the pure in heart," we might wonder who He is talking to. The good news is that He really is talking about us.

Christ ties purity of heart to something else that seems equally impossible: "for they shall see God"!

In the Old Testament, Moses wanted to see the glory of God, so God put him in a cleft of a rock. God's presence would pass by, but Moses would only be allowed to see the afterburn of God's glory. God said, "You cannot see my face, for man shall not see me and live" (Ex. 33:20).

Yet here Jesus says, "Blessed are the pure in heart, for they shall see God."

The apparent impossibility of these two things—seeing God and purity of heart—shows us how great a Savior Jesus Christ is. Christ does not speak these beatitudes to mock us. He comes as the great Redeemer, the Rescuer, the Savior. He is holding this wonderful promise in His hands: despite all the baggage that sinful habits leave in your thoughts, feelings, and desires, you can become pure in heart! You can be so completely forgiven, washed, and cleansed that when you see God, instead of shrinking back into an everlasting hell, you will move forward into the embrace of His everlasting love!

So although my first thought on reading this beatitude is, "This looks impossible," my second thought is, "But if I could lay hold of all that Christ promises here and make it my own, I would be greatly blessed."

MISUNDERSTANDINGS OF PURITY

Let's begin by clearing away the most common misconception. Purity of heart does not mean sinlessness of life. If it did, nobody would ever be pure in heart and nobody would ever see God. Christians in this life are always sinners in the process of recovery. We can grow and make progress, but none of us ever becomes all that God calls us to be, or even all that we could be in this life.

Scripture is very clear on this point. Writing to believers, John says, "If we say we are without sin, we deceive ourselves, and the truth is not in us" (1 John 1:8). So purity of heart does not mean you never have a bad thought. This should come as a relief to you as it does to me.

The Bible speaks about purity or holiness in different ways, and it is important for our understanding of the Christian life to distinguish between them.

First, there is the purity or holiness that belongs to God alone. In the presence of God, the holy angels, who have *never* sinned, cover their faces and cry out, "Holy, holy, holy is the Lord of hosts" (Isa. 6:3). It isn't enough, in the immediate presence of the Almighty, for the angels to say that God is holy. They say it three times, because while the angels themselves are holy, God is incomparable in His purity, and His holiness is the source of theirs.

Second, there is the purity or holiness that will be ours in heaven. "When he appears we shall be like him, because we shall see him as he is" (1 John 3:2). When you are in the presence of Jesus, there won't be a trace of sin in you, on you, or around you. You will reflect the purity of your Savior but you will do it as the moon reflects the light of the sun. Holiness is God's alone, and the purity that you will enjoy forever comes in its entirety from Him.

Third, there is a purity or holiness that God calls us to pursue now, and our Lord speaks of this in the sixth beatitude, "Blessed are the pure in heart, for they shall see God" (Matt. 5:8). Watson describes this as purity in a gospel-sense. "A face," he says, "may be said to be fair which has some freckles in it."[1] That analogy is profoundly helpful. A face may be beautiful without being perfect, and purity in a Christian is not perfection. The Christian's purity in this life is like gold mixed with dross. The gold is real and it has value even though it is not perfectly refined. Where there is a longing for purity and a loathing of impurity in the soul of a believer, there is a true expression of purity of heart.

WHAT PURITY OF HEART IS

So, if purity of heart doesn't mean sinlessness of life, what then does it mean? There are two answers to this question. The first is that a pure heart is an undivided heart.

An Undivided Heart

In his book *The Pilgrim's Progress*, John Bunyan has a character called "Mr. Facing Both Ways,"[2] who has been described by one writer as "the fellow with one eye on heaven and one on earth—who sincerely preaches one thing and sincerely does another, and from the intensity of his unreality, is unable to see or feel the contradiction."[3]

When Elijah gathered God's people at Mount Carmel and asked them how long they would continue "limping between two different opinions" (1 Kings 18:21), he was challenging them to purity of heart. God's people had been facing both ways. They wanted the blessings of God, but they kept giving themselves to idols. We need to hear the force of his challenge today. How long will you limp between two opinions? How long will you go on trying to embrace Christ and the world at the same time? How long will you continue toying with the same sins, never giving yourself to them completely, but never giving yourself wholly to Christ either?

A pure heart is an undivided heart and when Jesus says, "Blessed are the pure in heart" (Matt. 5:8), He pronounces a blessing on the man or the woman who is single-minded in following after Him.

Our Lord returns to this theme later on in the Sermon on the Mount. "The light of the body is the eye: if therefore [your] eye be single, [your] whole body shall be full of light" (Matt. 6:22 KJV). The ESV and NIV speak of the eye being healthy rather than single. "Healthy" is a clearer translation, but the word "single" is helpful because it communicates the idea of going after one thing. Picture an Olympic sprinter, laser focused on the finish line as he charges down the track. He does not even glance to the left or the right because he knows that the slightest movement will cost him that fraction of a second that could prove vital. His eye is single. The entire capacity of his mind and body is fully aligned in the pursuit of a single goal.

When Danish philosopher Soren Kierkegaard wrote a book entitled *Purity of Heart Is to Will One Thing,* his title faithfully reflected the teaching of Scripture, where a pure heart is contrasted with a divided heart: "Cleanse your hands, you sinners, and purify your hearts, you double-minded" (James 4:8). Notice that the opposite of a pure heart is to be double-minded, like Mr. Facing Both Ways.

David captured a believer's longing for purity when he prayed, "Teach me your way, O Lord, that I may walk in your truth; *unite my heart* to fear your name" (Ps. 86:11, emphasis added). That's a wonderfully helpful prayer. When you pray for purity, you can say, "Lord, my heart is all over the place, distracted, and pulled in different directions, and I am asking You to make it one. Unite my heart and make me a person who pursues one thing."

Paul gives us a window into his own pursuit of a pure heart when he writes, "One thing I do: forgetting what lies behind and straining forward to what lies ahead, I press on toward the goal for the prize of the upward call of God in Christ Jesus" (Phil. 3:13–14). Notice again that purity of heart is not perfection. Paul is very clear about this: "Not that I have already obtained this or am already perfect" (v. 12). Then, just in case you missed it, he says it again. "Brothers, I do not consider that I have made it my own" (v. 13).

Purity of heart is not perfection and it is not sinlessness of life. It is not even being where you would want to be in your growth as a Christian. After all the ways that Paul had extended himself in the service of Christ, even to the point of being in prison on account of his ministry while he wrote these words, he still felt that he had not yet become all that he wanted to be for Christ, let alone all that Christ was calling him to be. Purity of heart does not lie in what we attain but in what we pursue and in how we pursue it. Paul's "one thing I do" captures the singleness of purpose that characterizes the pure in heart. Purity of heart is to will one thing.

A Heart Forgiven

When you believe in the Lord Jesus Christ, faith forms the bond of a living union in which Christ becomes yours and you become His.

You are "in Christ" and Christ is in you. In that union, two marvelous gifts become yours.

The first is forgiveness, in which God drops all charges against you, and reconciles you to Himself so that you are no longer His enemy but His friend. The reason that you will enter heaven is *not* that you are without sin, but rather that God does not charge your sins against you. God charges your sins to the account of Jesus, in whom these sins were judged, punished, and atoned for through His sacrifice as our sin bearer on the cross. "The Lord has laid on him the iniquity of us all" (Isa. 53:6).

In Christ your debts have been paid in full, so that they will not and cannot be charged to you on the last day. This is the spectacular truth of justification. "Being justified by faith, we have peace with God through our Lord Jesus Christ" (Rom. 5:1).

It follows that Christians enter into heaven, not only on the basis of mercy, but also on the basis of justice. A just person would never demand payment for a bill that had already been settled, and our just God will not demand payment for sins that have already been atoned for. This is why John says that God is "faithful and just to forgive us our sins" (1 John 1:9). He emphasizes God's justice because he is pointing to the atonement in which Christ paid for our sins on the cross.

A Christian's confidence before God in life and in death does not rest on the quality of his or her Christian life, which will be patchy at best. Our confidence is in the character of God who is faithful and just, and the work of our Savior who has sealed our justification by paying our debt through the shedding of His blood on the cross.

A Heart Washed Clean

The second gift that belongs to all who are in Christ is cleansing, in which God washes your mind, heart, and life. Forgiveness and cleansing belong together. John says, "If we confess our sins, he is faithful and just to *forgive* us our sins and to *cleanse* us from all unrighteousness"

138

(1 John 1:9, emphasis added). Those God forgives He also cleanses, and those He cleanses He also forgives. These twin blessings belong to all who are in Christ, but there is an important difference between them. Forgiveness and reconciliation happen once. In Christ, you are a friend of God, and you do not become His enemy every time you sin. But cleansing is different. We need this on a continuing basis and we never get beyond our need of it in this life.

Faith in Jesus Christ can be defined as confidence in His ability to forgive and to cleanse through the power of His blood. Christ is able to wash the heart that has been messed up by greed, lust, pride, and any other sin, habit, or compulsion that you may care to name.

THE STRUGGLE TO BELIEVE GOD CLEANSES

I've met many people over the years who would say that they believe in a Christ who forgives, but they struggle to believe in a Christ who cleanses. Come and sit beside me in my office as we try to help a man who feels completely overwhelmed by the power of his past sins.

There is sadness in his eyes as he comes in and takes his seat. After a few moments of introduction and a prayer for the Lord's help, I ask him why he has come and how we can be useful to him. He leans forward and begins to speak slowly.

"Pastor, you have to realize that I've got baggage. Over the years I've seen things that I wish I had never seen and I have done things that I wish I had never done, and all of this has had an effect on my soul. My thinking, feeling, and desiring are all messed up. Patterns of twisted thinking have led to patterns of compulsive behavior and I can't get free. These things are *in me*, Pastor. I know that God forgives me, but I can't imagine ever being different, there's just too much baggage."

How can we help this person? I think the place to begin is by helping him to believe in the Lord Jesus Christ. Of course he will say that he does believe. He will say that he is a Christian and that he has been for many years. I don't doubt that, but listen carefully to what he is saying. He believes that God can forgive him, but he can't imagine ever being different. Our privilege in this conversation will be to point him to the Christ who not only forgives but also cleanses, and to help him see the ability of Christ to wash his mind and heart, making him clean.

As the conversation progresses, you are likely to hear some resistance. Our friend will insist that he does believe in the Lord Jesus Christ, and will want to move us on to some other line of discussion, but with gentle firmness, I will say to him, "As long as you persist in believing that nothing can be done about the baggage in your mind and in your heart, you do not yet know the Christ of the Bible, who washes, cleanses, and purifies messed-up human minds and hearts. You may say that you believe in a Jesus who forgives, but I am saying to you, that if you persist in this deeply held conviction that nothing can be done about the accumulated twistedness that has come from your past decisions and behaviors, you are not trusting the Savior who came not only to forgive your sins but also to wash your heart and your life. Christ cleanses messed-up minds, and hope will begin for you when you trust this Savior to purify your heart."

He's listening now, but if the truth is to settle in his mind, he needs to see it clearly in the Scriptures. So we turn to the Bible, starting at Matthew 1:21, "You shall call his name Jesus, for he will save his people from their sins." What does that mean? Our sins include habits, compulsions, and engrained patterns of thought and behavior. Christ came not only to save us from the guilt and consequence of our sins, but from the sins themselves. He came to deliver us from the power that they exercise over us, and every time I say the name Jesus, I am to remember this great truth that He came to save me from my sins.

Then we turn to Titus 3:5 where we read that God saves us "by the washing of regeneration and renewal of the Holy Spirit." Christ saves us by washing. He washes your mind and regenerates your heart. That means He gives you new affections, new interests, new inclinations, and new energy, so that over time you will find yourself hating the sin you used to love. As Christ washes your heart you will gain a fresh love for Him, a new interest in His Word, in His people, and in His service. The thoughts of your mind and the affections of your heart will change as Christ washes your soul. The sins that have held you in their grip will lose their power over you. Your defeats and failures will be fewer, and strength in your battle against temptation will become greater.

A STEPPING-STONE TO MOVING FORWARD

As you observe the man in my office learning to deal with his sins, you may also feel your need to be cleansed and freed from stubborn sins in your own life. If so, let me give you a stepping-stone that will help you to move forward. The beginning of faith is to say, "If I was in Christ, and He was in me, I believe He could make this heart clean."

If you feel that you cannot yet trust Christ to cleanse you, take this first step today: believe that He *could* make your heart clean. Christ changed the violent and blasphemous heart of Saul of Tarsus, making him a completely different person, and if He could do that for him, He could do the same for you. Settle this truth in your mind: *My heart could be made clean. I believe that if I was in Christ, and He was in me, He could make me clean.* Once you are on this stepping-stone of believing what Christ could do, you will be ready to take the next step and ask Him to do this for you.

ACTIVE LANGUAGE

When God purifies our hearts, He deals with the twisted patterns of our thinking, the misdirected patterns of our loving, and the engrained patterns of our behaving. God is the One who does this work of cleansing and sanctification (1 Thess. 5:23–24), but He calls us to be actively engaged in the process.

There is a distinction here that is important to grasp. In forgiveness, we come to the Lord empty-handed, and our only contribution to our justification is to receive by faith the gift that Christ offers. But when it comes to our sanctification, the position is different. As a believer in Christ you are not empty-handed. God's Spirit lives in you. You have a new heart, and God has put you in a position where, by His grace and in His strength, you are able to act. "In justification, our own works have no place at all, and simple faith in Christ is the one thing needful," wrote Bishop Ryle. "In sanctification our own works are of vast importance and God bids us fight, and watch, and pray, and strive and take pains, and labour."[4]

God calls us to be proactive in the pursuit of purity, and our role in this process is made clear in the writings of James, Paul, Peter, and John.

James says, "Draw near to God, and he will draw near to you. Cleanse your hands, you sinners, and purify your hearts, you double-minded" (James 4:8). Notice our active involvement: God draws near to us, but we are the ones who must purify our hearts. There is something for us to do here and God calls us to do it.

Paul uses similar language: "Since we have these promises, beloved, let us cleanse ourselves from every defilement of body and spirit, bringing holiness to completion in the fear of God" (2 Cor. 7:1). Notice the same pattern as we saw in James: God has given us His promise, and it is through His promise that we have hope of deliverance from sin. But God calls us to act in the light of His promise. We are to cleanse ourselves from every defilement of body and spirit. Nowhere in the Bible are we told that we must forgive ourselves, but here we read that we must cleanse ourselves.

Peter writes in the same way when he speaks of believers "having purified your souls by your obedience to the truth" (1 Peter 1:22). Again, the Bible never speaks of believers justifying themselves, but here God speaks about believers purifying themselves, indicating that we are actively engaged.[5] John uses the same language when he says, "Everyone who thus hopes in him [Christ] purifies himself as he [Christ] is pure" (1 John 3:3). These Scriptures and many others that speak of our active engagement in the struggle against sin lead to this clear conclusion: the pursuit of purity is a process in which God calls you to be actively engaged.

Have you ever wondered why it is that while some believers show marvelous evidence of growth, others seem only to become older versions of what they were before? Why is it that when some get free from the baggage of their past and master the sharp tongue or the fearful spirit, and leave behind the self-absorbed life, others seem to remain stuck in the same place with the same hang-ups and make very little progress?

I'm convinced that the answer often lies in a lack of clarity over our responsibility as believers to be actively engaged in the pursuit of purity, and a failure to practice on a sustained and consistent basis the things God has called us to do.

We have established that a pure heart is a heart that wills one thing and a heart that is washed clean. We have seen that God not only forgives but that He also cleanses and that this cleansing is the means by which He deals with the baggage of our lives. And having seen that God calls us to be actively engaged in the pursuit of purity, we turn now to seven practices that promote purity of heart.

SEVEN PRACTICES THAT
PROMOTE PURITY OF HEART

1. Believe: The Practice of Trusting Christ to Change You

Now may the God of peace himself sanctify you completely, and may your whole spirit and soul and body be kept blameless at the coming of our

Lord Jesus Christ. He who calls you is faithful; he will surely do it.
—1 Thessalonians 5:23–24

As we have seen, progress in the Christian life begins with *believing* that Christ can cleanse you. When you feel that your temptations are too strong, your failures are too many, your wounds are too deep, and your progress is too slow, look at the risen Savior who is able to cleanse you and put your trust in Him.

The Gospels record an occasion when Jesus and His disciples were crossing a lake in a boat. A storm blew up, and it was so severe that even the seasoned fishermen feared for their lives. Jesus calmed the storm by speaking a word that showed His authority even over the wind and the waves, and then He asked His disciples a question "Where is your faith?" (Luke 8:25). The disciples had faith in Jesus. They had left everything to follow Him. The problem was that they were not trusting Christ for the particular challenge of the storm they were facing.

So where do you need to exercise faith right now? Maybe it's in a struggle with pride or lust or fear. You have battled with this sin for many years and you have often felt defeated. But today Christ calls you to trust Him in your battle for purity. He is able to sanctify you, and He will, but He calls you to be actively engaged and that engagement begins with believing His promise of cleansing.

2. Confess: The Practice of Naming and Opposing Particular Sins

If we confess our sins, he is faithful and just to forgive us our sins and to cleanse us from all unrighteousness. —1 John 1:9

Notice that confessing and cleansing are closely related. When you set your mind to go after purity, you need to identify the sins from which you want your soul to be purified. In chapter 2, we looked at this in detail, but the place of confession in the pursuit of purity is so important that I must list it as a practice here.

What sins need to be hunted down in your soul in order for you to grow in purity? Are you hindered by a critical or sour spirit? Have you got into the habit of complaining and lost sight of thanksgiving? Are you held back from pursuing all that you could be for the Lord because of a timid or fearful spirit?

When you can name some sins that you are currently seeking to overcome, and ask for God's help to see them at their earliest approach—and to overcome them by *His* power—you will be well on your way to making significant progress in your pursuit of purity.

Our first calling in regard to confession is that we should confess our sins to God, but the Bible also speaks about the healing that can come when we confess our sins to each other: "Confess your sins to one another and pray for one another, that you may be healed" (James 5:16). James wrote these words in relation to a person who is sick calling for the elders of the church to pray for one's healing. So we should not use this verse to impose or imply a requirement on all believers to confess their sins to one another. Instead, this is an opportunity to embrace, especially when we are struggling in the pursuit of purity.

Relationships of trust where you are able to share the front lines of your battle against sin are a special gift from God, and you should make it your business to find a mature believer, or a small group of Christian friends, with whom you can be honest, knowing that they will pray with you, especially when you are struggling to gain victory over a stubborn sin in your life. But remember that James says to "pray for one another that you may be healed." Christ's design for the pursuit of purity is that we will help each other, and every Christian has something to give as well as to receive.

3. Listen: The Practice of Immersing Yourself in the Word of God

Christ loved the church and gave himself up for her, that he might sanctify her, having cleansed her by the washing of water with the word.
—Ephesians 5:25–26

Christ washes His people with the Word. Scripture is as essential to your pursuit of purity as water is to washing. This is why, when Christ prayed for His disciples, He said to the Father, "Sanctify them in the truth; your word is truth" (John 17:17), and why, when David asked, "How can a young man keep his way pure?" he answered, "By guarding it according to your word" (Ps. 119:9).

Over many years as a pastor, I have noticed this consistent pattern: the people whose lives have been significantly changed are like sponges absorbing the Word of God. They hide the Scripture in their hearts and it has a purifying effect on their lives. The entrance of God's Word "gives light" (Ps. 119:130), and when people make little or no progress, I have often found that there has been little entrance of the Word into their lives.

So as you pursue purity, immerse yourself in the Scriptures, knowing that the Word of God will have a cleansing effect in your life. Seize every opportunity for this. When you hear the Word preached, ask God to use it for the cleansing of your soul, and listen expectantly, applying what you hear as you believe what God says and obey what He commands.

Then establish a regular pattern of feeding on God's Word in private. I say feeding rather than reading because reading is not enough. James tells us that it is possible to look in the mirror of God's Word and go away unchanged (1:22–24). If you approach reading the Bible as an exercise, like working out on the treadmill, you will miss the nourishment that you could find. Feeding is more than reading. It involves reflecting, applying, believing, thanking, confessing, rejoicing, and committing in response to what God says in His Word.

Over time, the cumulative effect of immersing yourself in God's Word will be like the effect of soapy water on dirty clothes in a washing machine. As the machine agitates, the stain is slowly, gradually, and increasingly loosened from the fabric. Over time, the Word of God will have this cleansing effect even on the toughest stains in your life.

4. Worship: The Practice of Gazing on the Glory of God

We all, with unveiled face, beholding the glory of the Lord, are being transformed into the same image from one degree of glory to another.
—2 Corinthians 3:18

The above verse speaks directly to our central focus on growing in purity. Paul describes a person who is being "transformed" and he tells us that it happens as he or she beholds the glory of the Lord.

The day is coming when faith will be turned to sight, and we will see the Lord face-to-face, but that is not what Paul is describing here. He writes in the present tense and speaks of an ongoing process of change that happens in the lives of Christian believers as we worship. The principle is simple: becoming by beholding. The more you see of the glory of Christ, the more you will be transformed into His likeness.

Worship is more than attending a service at church on a Sunday morning. It is the gaze of the soul on the greatness and glory of God, and Paul tells us that beholding the glory of the Lord has a transforming effect in the life of a Christian believer.

If you are struggling with an addiction, or a behavior that has become habitual and compulsive, ask yourself, "How did I get here? How did this thing gain such power in my life?" Here's the answer: you made an idol of this thing, and you set your affections on the idol. You went to the idol for comfort, looked to it for happiness, and having set up the idol, you worshiped your way into this addiction. Now how are you going to get free from the power of this idol? You worshiped your way in and you must worship your way out. And you do that as you practice gazing on the glory of God.

The great promise attached to the sixth beatitude is that the pure in heart are blessed because they will see God. This marvelous promise relates not only to the joy we will have when we finally see Christ, but to glimpses of His glory that are given to the pure in heart in worship.

Purifying your heart will lead to seeing God, but the reverse also holds true: seeing God will lead to purifying your heart. This was Isaiah's experience. He had been serving the Lord for many years, speaking

GAINING MOMENTUM / Seven Practices That Promote Purity of Heart

1. *Believe.* This is the practice of trusting Christ to change your life. Christ is able to sanctify you, and He will, but He calls you to be actively engaged and that engagement begins with believing His promise of cleansing. When you feel your temptations are too strong and your progress too slow, look at the risen Savior and put your trust in Him.

2. *Confess.* This is the practice of naming and opposing particular sins. Ask for Christ's help to recognize each sin at its earliest approach; overcome the sin by *His* power. Also find a mature believer, or a small group of Christian friends, with whom you can be honest, knowing that the person or group will pray with you to gain victory over a stubborn sin in your life.

3. *Listen.* This is the practice of immersing yourself in the Word of God. Scripture is as essential to your pursuit of purity as water is to washing (Ps. 119:9). The Word of God can have a cleansing effect in your life. Establish a regular pattern of feeding on God's Word in private. Such feeding involves reflecting, applying, believing, thanking, confessing, and committing in response to what God says in His Word.

4. *Worship.* This is the practice of gazing on the glory of God. According to the apostle Paul, we become by beholding (2 Cor. 3:18). The more you see of the glory of Christ, the

the Word of God as a prophet during the long years of the reign of King Uzziah, but in the year that the king died, Isaiah was given a vision of the Lord and in seeing God's glory, he came to a new awareness of where he needed to grow in purity: "I am a man of unclean lips, and I dwell in the midst of a people of unclean lips" (Isa. 6:5).

Isaiah saw the glory of the Lord in a vision. Faith beholds the glory of the Lord in worship, and as we behold His glory we are changed into His likeness. If you have formed the habit of being passive when others are worshiping, taking the stance of a spectator and allowing your mind to wander when others in the congregation are singing, praying,

---

more you will be transformed into His likeness. Purifying your heart will lead to seeing God, but the reverse also holds true: seeing God will lead to purifying your heart. Beholding the glory of the Lord has a transforming effect in the life of a Christian believer.

5. *Ask.* This is the practice of praying for purity. Prayer gives you access to God at any time, but the prayer confessing your sin and being washed and forgiven can include the prayer of having, like King David, "a clean heart . . . and . . . a right spirit [renewed] within me" (Ps. 51:10). The prayer for a clean heart is a believer's prayer, and we should bring it often to the Lord.

6. *Persevere.* This is the practice of getting up when you have fallen down. Nobody makes uninterrupted progress on the path of purity. In the battle against personal sins, get up when you fall down. Remember, every time you say no to a sin, you weaken its power, and make your own position stronger.

7. *Anticipate.* This is the practice of knowing who you are and rejoicing in what you will be. You are forgiven and reconciled to the Father, and you have been adopted into the family of God. The Scriptures declare that when Christ returns, "[you] shall be like him," so "everyone who thus hopes in him purifies himself as he is pure" (1 John 3:3). Calling to mind who you are and what you shall be will help you in your pursuit of purity.

or submitting themselves to the Word, it's time to get serious about growing in purity as you enter into worship.

5. Ask: The Practice of Praying for Purity

Wash me, and I shall be whiter than snow. —Psalm 51:7

Psalm 51 is a wonderful prayer for purity. David felt that the guilt of his sin was clinging to him, and so he prayed, "Purge me with hyssop, and I shall be clean; wash me, and I shall be whiter than snow" (Ps. 51:7). His sin had taken the light and joy out of his life and so he prayed, "Let me hear joy and gladness; let the bones you have broken rejoice" (v. 8).

Prayer gives you a marvelous access to God at any time and in any circumstance, even when you feel trapped in the mire of your own sin and guilt. That's where David was when he prayed, but rather than give in to despair, he brought his guilt to the Lord and prayed for cleansing. We can come to the Lord in the same way, but when we do we have a great advantage over David. He knew that God would find a way to deal with sin, but we know that He has done this through the death and resurrection of His Son. David knew that God would find a way of washing him clean; we know that cleansing comes through the shed blood of Jesus Christ.

Notice that David asked for more than cleansing. After praying that the guilt and stain of his sin would be washed, purged, and removed, he then prayed, "Create in me a clean heart, O God, and renew a right spirit within me" (v. 10). David knew that he had been led into sin by the desires of his own heart and if his heart was not changed, it would not be long before that heart would once more lead him down the same sinful path.

The prayer for a clean heart is a believer's prayer, and we should bring it often to the Lord. When did you last ask God for a pure heart?

Watson says, "Most men pray more for full purses than pure hearts."[6] I don't know if that is true, but I am sure that more praying for purity of heart would lead to more progress toward that goal.

6. Persevere: The Practice of Getting Up When You Have Fallen Down

Rejoice not over me, O my enemy; when I fall, I shall rise; when I sit in darkness, the Lord will be a light to me. —Micah 7:8

Nobody makes uninterrupted progress on the path of purity. When you set yourself to battle against sins that have held sway in your heart, you will stumble and fall. The people who make progress in the Christian life are the ones who follow the exhortation of Micah and get up when they have fallen down.

The battle for purity is a long warfare, it's a marathon rather than a sprint, and perseverance is a key to success. John Owen said that sin will not die, "but by being gradually and constantly weakened; spare it, and it heals its wounds, and recovers strength."[7]

Every time you say yes to a sin, you increase its power in your life, making the next temptation harder to resist. But every time you say no to a sin, you weaken its power, and make your own position stronger. The power of sin is weakened little by little. That means you have to stay in the fight and win more rounds than you lose.

Think of your pursuit of purity in terms of a game of football. Every time you say no to sin you move the ball forward, and every time you say yes you lose yards and are back on defense. In any game, there will be times when you're on offense and times when you're on defense, and the game can be won or lost at either end of the field.

Always be careful when you are gaining yards in a drive. When you think you're doing really well, sin can snatch the ball and be in the end zone before you know it. And remember, when you have put points on the board, that's the time when you most need to be on your defense. When you are most blessed, sin will be coming back at you. But perhaps the most important lesson from the football metaphor is this: when sin has broken through your defenses and scored a touchdown, don't leave the field. This is not the time to quit. It's time for you to begin a new drive against sin in your life, so move the ball forward, and don't ever give up.

7. Anticipate: The Practice of Knowing Who You Are and Rejoicing in What You Will Be

We are God's children now, and what we will be has not yet appeared; but we know that when he appears we shall be like him, because we shall see him as he is. —1 John 3:2

Your enemy the devil will always try to remind you of who you were, but Christ tells you who you are. Forgiven and reconciled to the Father, you are a child of God. The love of the Father has been lavished on you. You have been bought with a price, and you have been adopted into the family of God. It's hard to sin willfully against love like that. But there's more. When you see Christ, you will be like Him, and John goes on to draw this conclusion: "everyone who thus hopes in him purifies himself as he is pure" (1 John 3:3).

Calling to mind who you are will help you in your pursuit of purity. When temptation comes, you can say, "That's not who I am. I am a dearly loved child of God, and by His grace I will press on." And calling to mind what you will be will help you when you have failed. Instead of becoming discouraged and dejected, you can say, "This is not the end for me. I belong to Christ and no child of His ends in failure. One day I will see Him and then I will be like Him; so by His grace I will get up and press on."

PURSUE PURITY

Some people have the idea that purity is something that you have when you are young, and you lose it if you mess up. That is the way the word "purity" is often used. But in the Bible purity is not something that you lose; it's something that you gain as you grow in the Christian life. It's not something behind you that was lost, but something ahead of you to be pursued and to be gained.

So go after purity. Be intentional about using each of these seven practices in your pursuit of a clean and undivided heart. The more you grow in purity, the more you will see God. You will see Him in His Word and in worship, you will see Him in your trials and in your triumphs, and you will see Him in His people and in His church. Your seeing will be with the eye of faith, and when He comes or calls, you will see Him face-to-face.

"Blessed are the peacemakers, for they shall be called sons of God."

MATTHEW 5:9

7

I GIVE UP
MY RIGHTS

THE GIFT OF MAKING PEACE

The fact that making peace is the last beatitude we are to pursue[1] tells us that it is of great importance to God, and that we should not be surprised when we experience difficulty in finding it. Everyone does.

Throughout these chapters, we have seen that there is order and progress in the Beatitudes, and as we have moved from ring to ring, we have found that the challenge becomes greater and we have to stretch further. Getting onto the last ring is not easy. You have to swing through all of the other rings that came before. Perhaps that is why peacemakers are hard to find. But having arrived at this chapter, it is time for the ultimate stretch, the highest and hardest of them all—to be a peacemaker in this world of conflict.

Psalm 55 records David's grief over broken relationships among God's people. When he said, "I see violence and strife in the city" (Ps. 55:9), he was speaking about the city of God, and the intensity of David's grief lay in the fact that the strife and violence did not come from invading armies. It arose among God's own people, and its roots lay within David's own family. His son Absalom had gathered a following of discontented people who rose up in rebellion against David, so that, at one point, David was driven from his palace in Jerusalem.

CONFLICT IN THE FAMILY

David loved his son, but he was unable to make peace with him. Absalom set his face against his father and refused to be reconciled, so the great king was left to lament the fracturing of his own family and the dividing of God's own people:

> It is not an enemy who taunts me—then I could bear it; it is not an adversary who deals insolently with me—then I could hide from him. But it is you, a man, my equal, my companion, my familiar friend. We used to take sweet counsel together; within God's house we walked in the throng. (Psalm 55:12–14)

Anyone who knows the grief of a trust being betrayed in a marriage, a business partnership, or a ministry will relate to the pain of David's words, "My companion stretched out his hand against his friends; he violated his covenant. His speech was smooth as butter, yet war was in his heart" (vv. 20–21). David's response to this betrayal is recorded in words that speak to every believer who faces the searing pain of a broken bond that could not be healed: "Cast your burden on the Lord, and he will sustain you; he will never permit the righteous to be moved" (v. 22).

Thomas Watson says, "Satan kindles the fire of contention in men's hearts and then stands and warms himself at the fire."[2] I find that a sobering picture. Satan stirs up strife, quarreling, conflict, and division in the hearts of men and once he gets the flames going, he warms himself at the contention that burns in the human heart.

CALLED TO SEEK PEACE

Peacemaking is not optional for those who belong to Christ. It is our calling (1 Cor. 7:15). That means we are to contribute to the peace of our families. Members of your family may love each other dearly; they may be at each other's throats; or they may not be speaking to each other. Whatever the situation, God's calling to you is that, to the best of your ability, you contribute to the peace of your family. If relationships in your family are healthy, your calling is to play your part in keeping it that way. If relationships in your family have become dysfunctional, your calling is to use whatever influence you might have to make it better.

The same principle applies in the church. God calls you as a member of the congregation where you worship and serve Him to play your part in maintaining the unity of the Spirit in the bond of peace (Eph. 4:3) and, if that peace has been lost, to do what you can to restore it. Again, this is not an option; it is a calling. The same is true when it comes to relationships in your workplace, at the school, and in your neighborhood.

Since peace is our calling from God, we should be intentional about pursuing it. "Those who plan peace have joy" (Prov. 12:20). Where there is no peace, our task is to consider the best ways to get there. Planning involves weighing options, considering outcomes, and laying out ordered steps in pursuit of a clearly defined goal.

The Hebrew word *shalom* (peace) that is used in the Bible is more than the absence of conflict, and includes the active enjoyment of all that is good. As you think about what you should say and do, consider what would promote the greatest good for your family, church, colleagues, neighbors, and friends.

Having recognized that peace is our calling, and having considered how best to pursue it, we are to "strive for peace with everyone" (Heb. 12:14). Peacemakers don't stop with plans. They plan the work and they work the plan. The word *strive* indicates effort, hard work, and perseverance poured into the pursuit of our God-given calling.

PEACE OF HEART FLOWS FROM PURITY OF LIFE

The starting point for anyone who wants to be a peacemaker is to have peace in his own heart and life. Peacemakers are people who can bring peace to others because they have it themselves. A person who lives with unresolved conflict in his or her own heart cannot bring peace to others.

Conflict seems to follow some people around. It goes *with* them because it lives *in* them. What fills you will spill out from you when other people bump into you. This is surely why Christian leaders are to warn a divisive person, and if he or she is unresponsive after a second warning, have nothing more to do with them (Titus 3:10). God's people are to watch out for those who cause divisions, and we are to avoid them (Rom. 16:17). If you hang out with a divisive person, his or her contentiousness will rub off on you. So avoid divisive people.

Throughout this book, we have seen that the Beatitudes form a continuum in which each of the blessings comes out of what went before. In this case, the blessing of peace arises directly from the pursuit of purity. James alludes to the connection when he describes the wisdom from above as "first pure, then peaceable" (James 3:17). There is a definite order there. Peace of heart flows from purity of life.

Purity of heart means to will one thing, and a person who has this singleness of purpose will be at peace. The impure person, by contrast, has a heart that is fundamentally divided. He or she wants contradictory things at the same time, and as long as that unresolved conflict rages, there can be no peace.

James develops this theme when he asks, "What causes quarrels and what causes fights among you?" The answer is: "Your passions [that] are at war within you" (James 4:1). Passions "at war" are at the core of the divisive person. The impure person is divided, and that is why he or she will often become divisive. If this person had come to a place of willing one thing, he or she would have a means of dealing with their passions, and the pursuit of purity would lead to peace. But without purity, peace cannot be found. This is why the Bible says, "There is no peace for the wicked" (Isa. 57:21). The wicked cannot have peace because they do not have purity. The more you pursue purity the more you will enjoy peace, and the more you give way to impurity the more conflicted and restless you will become.

WHY PEACEMAKERS ARE CALLED SONS OF GOD

"Sons of God" are people who reflect His likeness. We sometimes say, "Like father, like son," or "The apple does not fall far from the tree" when we see the similarity of character, habits, or behavior of a parent reproduced in a child. Similarly, when you are born of God, some likeness to your heavenly Father will be reflected in your life, and that will be seen, especially in making peace.

Peacemakers are called sons of God for four reasons. First, *peacemakers are like their Father who has peace in Himself.* He is "the God of peace" (Rom. 15:33; 1 Thess. 5:23; Heb. 13:20). At no time has there ever been the slightest hint of tension or conflict in God. The Father, the Son, and the Holy Spirit are one in purpose and one in love.

Our Lord Jesus Christ is described as "the Prince of Peace" (Isa. 9:6). When He came into the world, the angels said, "Glory to God in the highest, and on earth peace" (Luke 2:14). The Bible says that Christ is our peace (Eph. 2:14). He came into the world to make peace, and He did it by shedding His blood on the cross (Col. 1:19–20).

Similarly, the Holy Spirit is the Spirit of Peace. When Jesus was baptized, Matthew tells us that the Spirit of God descended on Him as "a dove" (Matt. 3:16), which is the symbol of peace.

When Jesus appeared to His disciples after the resurrection, He said, "Peace be with you. As the Father has sent me, even so I am sending you." Then He breathed on them and said to them, "Receive the Holy Spirit" (John 20:21–22). The connections are clear: the great Peacemaker gives peace to His disciples so that through the gospel they might bring to others what they themselves have received in the power of the Holy Spirit.

Second, *peacemakers are like God because they surrender their rights.* God the Son did not hold on to what was His by right. He left heaven. He stepped down and He came into the world for us in order to make peace. Martyn Lloyd-Jones says: "If God stood upon his rights and dignity, upon his person, every one of us . . . would be consigned to hell and absolute perdition."[3]

We live in a world of rights, and there may be times when it is appropriate to insist on them. But before you insist on your rights in a situation of conflict, remind yourself that if God had stood on His rights, you would be in hell forever and so would everyone else. You don't make peace by standing on your rights.

Third, *peacemakers are like God because they move toward trouble.* I once heard a consultant say that in dealing with conflict it is important to "move toward the barking dog." I don't know about you, but that is never my inclination! If a dog is barking, my instinct is to back off. But when the world was barking at God, He did not back off. He moved toward us, even though He knew it would lead to the cross.

Peacemaking does not mean avoiding conflict. In fact, peacemakers often cause a great deal of trouble in the pursuit of peace. I believe this is what Jesus was referring to when He said, "I have not come to bring peace, but a sword" (Matt. 10:34). Christ came to make peace between men and God. He moved toward the problem, but when He came, trouble flared. That will often be the experience of a peacemaker.

Peacemaking is not for the fainthearted; it takes courage. It could be the most dangerous job in the world. For Jesus it meant laying down His life.

Fourth, *peacemakers are like God* because *they love others before they are loved in return*. Paul put it this way: "God shows his love for us in that while we were still sinners, Christ died for us" (Rom. 5:8).

Putting all of this together may make you feel, as I do, that any resemblance between us and the Lord is very slight indeed. This, of course, is true in regard to our pursuit of all the Beatitudes. Our progress in purity, our mercy toward others, our hunger for righteousness, our submission to God's will, our mourning over sin, and our awareness of our own needs all fall a long way short of what we would want them to be, and much farther short of what God calls us to be. We may grow and make progress, but to the end of our lives we will always be sinners who depend on the grace and mercy of God. In this regard, it will be helpful to consider the aims, limits, and possibilities of progress in the Christian life.

AIMS, LIMITS, AND POSSIBILITIES

Many years ago, I found a little book by Bishop Handley Moule called *Thoughts on Christian Sanctity*.[4] Not the most exciting title, but in the nineteenth century people were wise enough to choose books by the author rather than the title. I'll always be grateful to the mentor who told me, "*Who* you read matters more than *what* you read." Read authors who are following hard after God.

The word "Sanctity" in Moule's title relates to sanctification or growth in the Christian life, which has been the theme of this book. Sanctification is a journey in which every Christian makes progress, but no Christian completes the journey in this life. Over the years, I have met more Christians who are troubled over sanctification than over any other Christian doctrine. Some fail to make progress because they do not have a clear vision of how they could change or what they could become. Others see what God is calling them to be, but they feel crushed by their own lack of progress. This is an area in which we desperately need balanced biblical thinking, and that is what I got from Bishop Moule.

The first chapter of his book is titled: "Aims, Limits and Possibilities." Under "Aims" he wrote, "It is nothing less than the supreme aim of the Christian Gospel, that we should be holy."[5] In particular, Moule says that we aim "to displace . . . self from the inner throne, and to enthrone Him; to make not the slightest compromise with the smallest sin. . . . to walk with God all day long; to abide every hour with Christ, . . . to love God with all the heart, and our neighbor as ourselves."[6]

These are the aims, but we pursue them knowing that there will be limits to what we actually attain. Here Moule says,

> I mean . . . not limits in our aims, for there must be none, nor limits in divine grace itself, for there are none, but limits, however caused, in the actual attainment by us of Christian holiness. There will be limits to the last, and very humbling limits, very real fallings short. To the last, it will be a sinner who walks with God.[7]

David knew the painful limits of his own peacemaking when he found that, despite his best efforts, he was not able to reconcile with his own son. There will be limits to our peacemaking, as there are limits to our purity, mercy, righteousness, meekness, mourning, and humility in this world. This is why Paul says, "If it is possible, as far as it depends on you, live peaceably with all" (Rom. 12:18). There will be situations where you cannot make peace, but don't let that stop you from trying. Don't quit the journey just because you may not be able to reach the end of the road.

That leads us to possibilities, and here Moule speaks of how it is possible, through the Lord's power, to live a life in which God's promises are found to be true, to find peace in the midst of pressure by casting every care on Him, to have affections and imaginations purified through faith, and to see the will of God in everything "not with a sigh, but with a song."

Aims, limits, and possibilities give a good framework for understanding the Christian life. If you forget the limits, you will find that you are constantly chiding yourself for your lack of progress. If you lose sight of the possibilities, you will default to accepting yourself as you are, and little progress will be made. Here's what you need for a balanced, biblical approach to sanctification: Embrace the aim! Recognize the limits! Go after the possibilities!

All of this is beautifully expressed in a prayer by Robert Murray M'Cheyne: "Lord, make me as holy as it is possible for a pardoned sinner to be made."[8] When it comes to peacemaking, you could pray, "Lord, let me bring peace as far as possible for a pardoned sinner in this fallen world." Moule also offers a helpful prayer: "Thou, Lord who knowest my heart, all its desire and all its need, show me what Thou art able to do with it, and do what Thou art able, through Jesus Christ Amen."[9]

SEVEN TACTICS FOR PEACEMAKERS

So you want to be a peacemaker. How would you go about it? What does peacemaking look like in practice and how is it best pursued? Here are seven tactics that you can deploy in the pursuit of peace.

1. Recognize where there is a problem.

They have healed the wound of my people lightly, saying, "Peace, peace," when there is no peace. —Jeremiah 6:14

There were, in the days of Jeremiah, as there are today, people who made a living from telling others that all is well. They said what people

163

wanted to hear and the effect of their ministry was like putting a Band-Aid over an infected wound. They healed the wounds of God's people lightly, and that made the problem worse.

Making peace does not mean avoiding conflict. It's not "anything for a quiet life." A conflict avoided is often a conflict postponed, and therefore a conflict that ultimately becomes worse. Kent Hughes believes that avoiding conflict is "particularly a male tendency." Speaking about marriage and family, he writes, "Even in our most intimate relationships, men tend to act as if everything is OK when it is not. Men often avoid reality because they want peace. But their avoidance heals the wound only slightly and prepares the way for greater trouble."[10]

Peacemaking begins with the honesty and courage that will recognize a problem and face it. Without this, no further progress can be made. When God makes peace with a person, He begins by wakening that person up to the fact that there is a problem in their relationship with Him. Think about how that happened in your life: at some point, you saw that things were not right between you and God. This was the work of God's Spirit and it was the beginning of His peacemaking work in your life. So the first step in making peace is admitting that there is a problem, and having the courage to face it.

2. Deal with conflict early.

The beginning of strife is like letting out water, so quit before the quarrel breaks out. —Proverbs 17:14

Growing up, I remember going to camp in the Scottish countryside. One day we decided to build a dam in a stream that was flowing down the hillside near to the place where we were staying. The idea was simple: block the stream and we would create a pool of water deep enough for a swim. It took some time to gather the stones and put them in place, but eventually the dam was built. Success! The pool was formed and the level of the water began to rise. Time to get ready for a swim! But there was a problem. A small trickle of water had found its way through the rocks. Before long the trickle had moved a few small stones, letting through more water, which then had the force to remove some larger stones. What began as a trickle ended in a flood. Our dam was swept away, the pool emptied, and all of our work was lost.

This is the picture that God gives us in Proverbs: the beginning of strife is like the first trickle of water. In any relationship that ends in acrimony, there is a moment when the strife begins. the people involved may not notice it, but there is a time when it begins. It may be the first harsh word, the first wound, or the first moment of distrust. It may not seem like much at the time, but the end is in the beginning. Later the people involved know that if they could go back and do it all over again, the outcome could be different.

But you can't go back, so deal with conflict early. Don't let small resentments take root because, if you do, they will grow. The beginning of strife is like letting out water, so quit before the quarrel breaks out.

3. Practice restraint, especially with your tongue.

Let every person be quick to hear, slow to speak, slow to anger. —James 1:19

Self-expression is one of the leading idols in our culture. "I *must* say what I think and feel!" Really? Are you sure that you *have* to? What would happen if you didn't?

Peacemakers practice restraint. When a relationship is under strain there may be times when you are tempted to unload, but if you are a peacemaker, you will hold back. Recognizing a problem and having the courage to face it does not mean letting rip with your accumulated frustrations, disappointments, and complaints. Too often I have seen attempts at peacemaking fail because one party felt that they had to lay out the entire history of every accumulated failure and grievance.

If God unloaded, at one time, every way in which you have wronged Him, you would be completely devastated. But God does not do that. He reveals your sins and failings slowly, gradually, and increasingly over time. He does this because He is the great Peacemaker and because He is full of grace as well as truth.

Let the way that God has dealt with you guide you in your pursuit of peace with others. Practice restraint, *especially* in relation to your tongue. Even in honest confrontation, you don't need to unload everything, and if you are a peacemaker, you won't.

4. Prepare for a long journey.

Seek peace and pursue it. —1 Peter 3:11

GAINING MOMENTUM / Seven Tactics for Peacemakers

1. *Recognize where there is a problem.* Making peace begins when you have the honesty to recognize a problem and then face it. Conflict may well follow such recognition, but the honesty in seeing its existence is the only way true peace can eventually follow.

2. *Deal with conflict early.* The first harsh word or the first moment of distrust may not seem like much at the time. Later, however, the people involved know that if they could go back to the beginning and do it all over, the outcome could be different. Don't let small resentments take root. If you do, they will grow.

3. *Practice restraint, especially with your tongue.* Recognizing a problem and having the courage to face it does not mean you have to dump your accumulated frustrations and complaints on the offender. God does not do that. As the great peacemaker, He reveals your sins and failings slowly, gradually, and increasingly over time. Remember, in honest confrontation you don't need to unload everything. As a peacemaker, you won't.

4. *Prepare for a long journey.* If you are called to be a peacemaker in a situation where wounds are deep, be prepared for the long haul. Peter writes we are to "seek peace

If you are serious about peacemaking, you may need to prepare for a long journey. It need not always be like this, and if the problem is recognized early, peace may be restored quickly. But if you are called to be a peacemaker in a situation where wounds are deep, you should be prepared for the long haul.

When Peter uses the word "seek," he is telling us that sometimes peace will not be easy to find. When he calls us to pursue it, he reminds us that peace may sometimes be far in the distance, and that to find it, we will need to stay on the journey. Peacemaking is a process, not an event.

When God made peace with us, He sought and pursued those who

---

and pursue it" (1 Peter 3:11); in seeking, he implies sometimes peace will not be easy to find. In his call to pursue it, he reminds us that peace may sometimes be in the distance. Peacemaking is a process, not an event.

5. *Take a step toward peace.* Sometimes the other person has no interest in making peace. A simple—or major—act of kindness is one step in her direction that may open that interest, show your goodwill, and put a crack in the wall of hostility.

6. *Aim at humility, not humiliation.* Peacemaking always calls for humility. When God made peace, He came to us in Jesus Christ. Jesus the Son took flesh, and spoke with His enemies face-to-face. He did not come with a display of strength, but chose to make Himself vulnerable. Peacemakers aim at *humility* . . . but never *humiliation.*

7. *Entrust to God any injustice you have suffered.* At times when you have evil returned for good, you may want to abandon your efforts at restoring peace. When that happens, trust God, even as Jesus did. Christ "continued entrusting himself to him who judges justly" (1 Peter 2:23). Christ, the great Peacemaker, left us an example so that we "might follow in his steps" (v. 21). Trusting yourself to God means letting Him deal with the injustice rather than trying to deal with it by vindicating yourself.

were "far off" (Eph. 2:13). Think about the length of the journey God took to be at peace with us! The root of our alienation from God goes all the way back to our first parents who sinned in the garden of Eden and then passed on the impulse to sin all the way down to you and me. We were born into a world that is *hostile* to God, and that hostility was in us by nature.

The process of God making peace with you goes back to the beginning of time. It took all the promises of the Old Testament, all the work of redeeming Israel, and all the ministry of sending the prophets. It took the coming of Christ into the world, His perfect fulfillment of all that God requires, His atoning death as the sacrifice for your sins, His rising from the dead, and His ascending into heaven. It took the sending of the Holy Spirit, who awakened you to your need of Christ, caused you to be born again, applied the full effect of the cleansing blood of Jesus to your life, and adopted you into the family of God! That is a long journey! God has been relentless in pursuing peace with us, and peacemakers reflect His persistence.

5. Take a step toward peace.

If your enemy is hungry, feed him; if he is thirsty, give him something to drink.
—Romans 12:20

Making peace may be a long journey, but even a long journey begins with a single step. When Paul speaks about "your enemy," he is describing a relationship where peace is a long way off. Your enemy regards you with hostility and may show no interest whatsoever in pursuing peace. And if another person has no interest in making peace, what can you do?

Even your enemy has needs, and Paul describes a situation where your enemy has a need for food. He or she is hungry, and that gives you the opportunity to show an act of kindness by giving this person something to eat. The principle here is a very simple one: when peace seems a long way off, think about what might be one small step in the right direction.

What could you do that would be well received by the person who is hostile toward you? Is there an act of kindness you can show, an evidence of goodwill you can display? What would be one step that would make this better, one step that might make another step possible?

I have long been fascinated by the story of the Cuban Missile Crisis, the moment when the world was on the brink of a nuclear holocaust. In 1962, two mighty nations were standing toe-to-toe, with powerful nuclear arsenals on either side. The Soviet Union had placed nuclear missiles in Cuba, just ninety miles from US shores. The United States enacted a naval blockade of the island nation and warned Cuba of a military attack if the ballistic missiles were not dismantled. The world held its breath and watched. To this day, the missile crisis remains among the most dangerous moments in the history of the world.

The great question at the heart of the Cuban Missile Crisis was simple: What could be done to begin a process of de-escalation? What would be *one step* that might ease the tension and allow the other side to respond by taking another step back from the brink of mutual destruction?

Now, think about a situation of conflict in your own life. What would be one step that you could take that might make another step by the person or people with whom you are in conflict possible?

6. Aim at humility, not humiliation.

Being found in human form, he humbled himself. —Philippians 2:8

God makes peace, not through a triumph of power, but through a triumph of love. He wins us because He woos us and draws us, and He does this despite the fact that all the right is on His side and all the wrong is on ours. That took extraordinary humility. Christ humbled Himself by taking human form and, as if that were not enough, He then humbled Himself by serving others rather than seeking to be served, which was His right.

Peacemaking always calls for humility. When God was giving the law, His voice thundered from Sinai. The effect of this thundering was that God's people were terrified and remained at a distance from Him. If Christ had not come, this would still be our position: complete alienation from a wholly righteous God.

Thundering emails or speeches when you deliver a piece of your mind will not move you nearer to peace. Impersonal communication rarely leads to personal reconciliation. When God made peace, He came to us in Jesus Christ. He took flesh, and spoke with His enemies face-to-face. He did not come with a display of strength, but chose to make Himself vulnerable. Think about your own experience of coming to Christ: was it not His love that drew you? When you came to Him, He did not rub your nose in the dirt of your own failure. No, He forgave you and He embraced you. That's what peacemakers do.

Peacemakers aim at *humility* . . . but never *humiliation*. When you've been wronged, it is important to ask yourself what you want to achieve. Do you want vengeance? Do you want vindication? Or do you want to make peace? If you want to see someone who has hurt you grovel in the dust, you are not yet ready to be a peacemaker. And if your aim is to demonstrate that you were right in what you said and did, you are not yet ready to make peace.

In his book about the Cuban Missile Crisis, Robert Kennedy quotes the words of his brother President John F. Kennedy, at the height of the crisis on October 26, 1962: "If anybody is around to write after this, they're going to understand that we made every effort to find peace and . . . give our adversary room to move. I'm not going to push the Russians an inch beyond what's necessary."[11]

The president's goal was peace, not vindication and not vengeance. If he had wanted vindication, he could have pressed for a public admission of wrongdoing. If he had wanted vengeance, he had plenty of firepower available. But by keeping the goal of peace in view, he was kept from straying down these dead-end and deadly paths.

When, after thirteen tension-filled days, the crisis was finally resolved, Robert Kennedy records that "after it was finished . . . he [the president] instructed all members of the . . . government that no interview should be given, no statement made, which would claim any kind of victory."[12] Why? Peacemakers aim at humility, but never humiliation.

7. Entrust the injustice you have suffered to God.

For this is a gracious thing, when, mindful of God, one endures sorrows while suffering unjustly. —1 Peter 2:19

Sometime in your life, you will experience the sorrow that comes from being slighted, treated unfairly, passed over, or taken for granted. It is a painful thing to have evil returned for good or to give of yourself and receive wounds in return. When you suffer unjustly, you need to know that Jesus has been there. No one was ever wronged and no one has ever had their rights ignored or flouted more than your Savior.

Yet Christ was the great Peacemaker and He endured the evils and injustices that were committed against Him as an example for us so that we "might follow in his steps" (1 Peter 2:21). This is a place to pause and reflect because God is speaking to us about how peacemakers act when we are wronged, provoked, or wounded.

First, "when he was reviled, he did not revile in return" (1 Peter 2:23). To revile means to use abusive language. Christ was subjected to what we would call today physical and verbal abuse. People insulted Him, spat on Him, and provoked Him. But when Jesus was reviled, He did not revile in return, and the reason was that He came to make peace.

When people speak to you in a demeaning or insulting way, your first instinct may be to pay them back in kind. But Peter tells us that Christ left us an example at precisely this point, so that we may follow in His steps (v. 21). Peacemakers absorb insults and hold back from returning them.

Second, "when he suffered, he did not threaten" (v. 23). Soldiers flogged Jesus, inflicting unimaginable pain on Him. He was the Son of God, and all judgment had been trusted to Him by the Father. Christ could easily have threatened judgment on His enemies. But He did not do that. Why? Because He came to make peace.

How was Christ able to do this, and how would it be possible for ordinary people like you and me to do the same? Christ "continued entrusting himself to him who judges justly" (v. 23). Trusting yourself to God means looking to Him to deal with the injustice rather than trying to deal with it by vindicating yourself.

Notice that Jesus continued entrusting Himself to the Father. He kept doing this during these agonizing hours on the cross. When you are wronged, the pressure and impulse to seek vindication for yourself will keep coming to you, and the only way to respond to that is to keep committing yourself to God who judges justly.

Knowing that He could trust the Father for His own vindication, and knowing that no evil could ever stop the Father's purposes for His life from being fulfilled, Jesus was able to do the hardest thing of all: "He himself bore our sins in his body on the tree" (1 Peter 2:24). This is one of the greatest statements of the atonement in the Bible. It describes the mystery of what Christ did for us, and what only Christ could ever do. But even here, in the uniqueness of Christ's work as our sin-bearer, we are being told that, in some sense, there is an example for us (v. 21).

When Christ bore our sins, He absorbed the pain of what we did to Him without passing it on. This, again, is what peacemakers do. Conflicts escalate when a person or people who are wronged retaliate, and their retaliation provokes a response. The only way for escalating cycles of retaliation to be broken is for someone to absorb the pain rather than pass it on. Someone has to say, "It stops here." This is what Christ, the great Peacekeeper, has done for us. Knowing that His vindication was with God, and trusting Him for the outcome, He broke the otherwise endless cycle of violence and vengeance by bearing our sins and absorbing the pain.

Paul speaks about becoming like Christ in His suffering, and Peter in these verses spells out what this means. To be like Christ in His suffering means that when you are reviled you do not answer in kind, and when you suffer you do not make threats. The only way that this is possible is to trust the injustice you have endured, the loss you have incurred, and the pain you have suffered into the hands of God your Father. When you know that your vindication is with Him and that no evil can ever thwart the fulfillment of His great purpose for your life, you will be able to absorb the pain rather than pass it on. In doing this, you will become a peacemaker.

"Blessed are those who are persecuted for righteousness' sake, for theirs is the kingdom of heaven. Blessed are you when others revile you

and persecute you and utter all kinds of evil against you falsely on my account. Rejoice and be glad, for your reward is great in heaven."

MATTHEW 5:10–12

8

I ENDURE THE COST

THE PRICE AND REWARD OF A GODLY LIFE

The eighth beatitude is different from all of the others. The first seven describe the life that God calls us to pursue: We are to cultivate a poverty of spirit that mourns over our sins and meekly submits to the will of God. These roots will produce a hunger and thirst for righteousness, and where this life grows, the fruit of mercy, purity, and peace will follow. We are to go after these things and pursue them with passion. We cannot ever get too much of them.

The last beatitude is different, because it describes the outcome of such a life. What should you expect as you move forward in the pursuit of godliness? Our Lord identifies two outcomes: you will be persecuted by the world and you will have great reward in heaven.

Persecution for righteousness' sake began in the first family. Adam and Eve had two sons and, like any other parents, they would have hoped that the two boys would grow up to be the best of friends. But Cain fought with his brother and killed him because "his own deeds were evil and his brother's righteous" (1 John 3:12). So Abel was killed "for righteousness' sake." He died because Cain, whose deeds were evil, hated the light that he saw in his brother's life. The second man to be born into the world died at the hands of the first, and his blood was shed on account of his faith.

FROM MOSES TO PAUL—ALL PERSECUTED

This harassment and persecution of believers did not end with Abel. Joseph was persecuted by his brothers, and later he was thrown into prison because he pursued purity in the house of Potiphar (Gen. 37, 39). Moses was rejected by the people he led (Ex. 17). Elijah was despised and persecuted (1 Kings 18–19), Nehemiah was opposed and defamed (Neh. 4), Jeremiah was thrown into a cistern (Jer. 38), Daniel was sent to a lion's den (Dan. 6), and his three friends were thrown into a fiery furnace (Dan. 3).

In the New Testament, John the Baptist was beheaded (Matt. 14), Stephen was stoned (Acts 7), Peter and John were imprisoned (Acts 12; Rev. 1), and Paul endured a relentless series of persecutions that spanned the entire course of his ministry (2 Cor. 11:16–33).

The antagonism that was focused first on the leaders of the early church spilled over into the lives of its members. To the congregation at Philippi, Paul wrote, "It has been granted to you that for the sake of Christ you should not only believe in him but also suffer for his sake" (Phil. 1:29). To the church at Thessalonica that was birthed in persecution he said, "We ourselves boast about you in the churches of God for your steadfastness and faith in all your persecutions and in the afflictions that you are enduring" (2 Thess. 1:4). In the same way, Peter, writing to believers scattered in Pontus, Galatia, Cappadocia, Asia, and Bithynia, says, "Do not be surprised at the fiery trial when it comes upon you to test you, as though something strange were happening to you" (1 Peter 4:12).

So when you are opposed, harassed, belittled, slandered, or even physically persecuted on account of your pursuit of a godly life, you do not need to ask, "Why is this happening to me?" Suffering for being a Christian is normal and we should expect it. This is the common experience of our brothers and sisters throughout the world (1 Peter 5:5), and "all who desire to live a godly life in Christ Jesus will be persecuted" (2 Tim. 3:12). Those who follow Christ will be blessed by God and hated by the world. There don't seem to be any exceptions.

THE ROOTS OF PERSECUTION

The roots of persecution lie in the hostility of the human heart toward God. The sinful nature is hostile to God (Rom. 8:7). Not neutral—hostile! Sinners hate God and when God's people grow in His likeness, they also will be hated. The One who is the perfect image of God, the exact representation of His being, suffered more than any other when He came into the world, and Jesus said to His disciples, "'A servant is not greater than his master.' If they persecuted me, they will also persecute you" (John 15:20).

When God's people are cold, confused, and compromised, reflecting little of their Father, the world will often ignore them, but when Christians get serious about pursuing righteousness, mercy, purity, and peace, they will get under the skin of godless people and soon find themselves facing trouble.

People who do evil hate the light (John 3:20). So if the light is in you, don't expect to be loved by the world. A sinner has to suppress his own conscience to sustain his continued resistance to God, and when you pursue a godly life you make this more difficult, as the light of Christ, which the sinner is trying to avoid, is reflected through you. So don't expect to be thanked for living a godly life in business, industry, or education. The world tolerates Christians with suspicion at best and persecutes us with hostility at the worst.

It is difficult to get accurate numbers of Christians who are persecuted for openly professing faith in Christ. One of the more conservative estimates is that nearly four thousand believers worldwide are killed for their faith each year. That is about ten Christians killed every day. Other forms of violence, such as, beatings, abductions, rapes, arrests, and forced marriages, are regularly committed against Christians, along with the destruction of over 2,500 Christian properties each year.[1]

For most of us, the cost of following Christ will not extend to laying down our lives, being imprisoned, or suffering physical violence. Thomas Watson helpfully distinguishes two forms of persecution: persecution of the hand, which may involve intimidation, violence, and even death, and persecution of the tongue, to which our Lord refers when He says that people will "revile you" and "utter all kinds of evil against you falsely on my account" (Matt. 5:11).

Persecution with the tongue may involve insults, false accusations, slander, and ridicule. It starts early. If you are known to be a Christian in high school, you should expect opposition. If you are committed to a path of purity and hold back from the sexual experimentation that has become a normal part of high school culture, people will think you strange and may even mock you.

SHOULD I STAY OR SHOULD I GO?

The easiest way to avoid pain, trouble, conflict, or opposition is to move on whenever it appears. Although that may be your first instinct, the teaching of Jesus in this eighth beatitude should make you cautious about defaulting to this approach.

Commenting on our culture of choice, Ajith Fernando says,

Somehow there seems to be this idea that if you are suffering you are doing something wrong. The problem is compounded by the mobility of affluent people today. As people keep changing from job to job, from neighborhood to neighborhood, and from church to church, long-term commitments are becoming a culturally rare phenomenon. . . . People are used to moving from place to place based on convenience, on the opportunity to be more productive, and on escaping from suffering and unpleasant relationships . . . [But] persevering through inconvenience, struggling to be productive against so many odds, taking on suffering, sticking to unpleasant relationships are what combine to produce great mission.[2]

This caution is surely wise and insightful. Moving on whenever trouble appears on the horizon is a formula for perpetual spiritual infancy. Nothing of value was ever accomplished without pressing on through difficulty, so don't take opposition, pressure, frustration, disappointment, or fear as an indication that it is time to move on. Peter Marshall said it well: "Oaks grow strong in contrary winds and diamonds are made under pressure."[3]

But is it sometimes right to seek an easier path? If your children are harassed at school, should you take them out of the program? When you face conflicts at work, is it time to move on? Are there times when fleeing from persecution is the right thing to do? If so, when? And how would you know? These are complex questions, and as Christians face increasing harassment, there will be a growing need for wise and biblical counsel.

The place to begin is with the clear instruction of our Lord: "Behold, I am sending you out as sheep in the midst of wolves, so be wise as serpents and innocent as doves" (Matt. 10:16). Notice, Christ does not say, "The world is like a pack of wolves ready to tear you apart, so go ahead and let them do it." Instead, He tells us that, in the light of the hostility and danger we will face in the world, we must be as wise as serpents and as innocent as doves. "Wise as serpents" means that we must be shrewd, learning to speak and act in the light of the threats and dangers we may face, and "innocent as doves" means that we must be careful not to speak or act in a way that would unnecessarily provoke others to do us harm.

Christ also gave His disciples great freedom when they faced opposition. "When they persecute you in one town, flee to the next" (Matt. 10:23). On one occasion, early in the ministry of Jesus, the people of Nazareth brought Him to the brow of a hill so that they could throw Him over the edge of a cliff. Rather than give Himself up to them, Christ passed "through their midst" and "went away" (Luke 4:30). Even our Lord could only die once, and before He gave His life there was work for Him to do. So we see in our Lord's example both a readiness to lay down His life and a readiness to move to a place of greater safety. Both the Savior's life and His teaching make it clear there are times when Christians should stay in the face of trouble and times when they should go.

But how do you discern this difference? How do you know when you should stand in the face of opposition, and when you should move on because of it?

The Wise Counsel of John Bunyan

John Bunyan (1628–88) deals with this question in his book *Seasonable Counsel, or Advice to Sufferers*. Bunyan knew what it was to face persecution and, having made tough decisions in the light of it, he was well positioned to offer this counsel.

Bunyan lived during the reign of Charles II (1660–85), which proved to be an especially difficult time for Baptist, Congregational, and other independent ministers and their churches in Britain. Charles wanted to create one unified church structure throughout the country and, with this in view, demanded that all ministers should be ordained by Anglican bishops and that all congregations should worship according to the Church of England liturgy. Those, like John Bunyan, who refused to submit to this demand were known as "nonconformists."

Bunyan was arrested in November 1660 while preaching to a gathering of believers at a farm close to Bedford. Some friends offered to post bail for him, but when they heard that the conditions of his release included that he should no longer preach, they knew that their money would be at risk, and withdrew their offer.[4] So Bunyan remained in prison for two months, when he was formally charged with encouraging unlawful assemblies and not conforming to the national worship of the Church of England.

At the trial, the judge laid out the choice for Bunyan in the starkest terms. If he would give up preaching and attend the authorized worship of the Church of England, he could be free after serving a three-month sentence for the offense to which he had pled guilty. But if he would not leave his preaching, the prospects were grim: "You must be banished from the realm; and after that, if you shall be found in this realm without special license from the king, you must stretch by the neck for it."[5]

Bunyan faced a tough decision. At the time of his arrest, he was thirty-two years old, married with four children, the eldest of whom was blind. He was under no obligation to continue preaching and could easily have chosen to pursue other work and honor Christ with a less public testimony. But Bunyan felt sure that God had called him to preach and so on hearing the terms of his release, he said to the judge, "I am at a point with you: If I were out of prison today, I would preach the gospel again tomorrow, by the help of God."[6] That landed him in prison for twelve years, and it was during that time that he wrote *The Pilgrim's Progress*.

Bunyan wrote movingly of the personal cost that his imprisonment would bring to his wife and children as well as to himself. "Parting with my wife and poor children has often been to me like pulling the flesh from my bones, not only because of all that they mean to me, but also because I have thought so much of many hardships, miseries, and wants that they were likely to meet, were I taken from them." The special needs of his blind daughter were particularly heartbreaking for him. "I

181

saw that I was as a man who was pulling down his house upon the head of his wife and children, yet I thought, I must do it. I must do it."[7]

You might expect that a man with courage like this would call others to take the harder path, but Bunyan's counsel to believers facing harassment is wonderfully tender and spiritually wise. In the light of the words of our Lord, "When they persecute you in one town, flee to the next" (Matt. 10:23), Bunyan said,

> You may do this even as it is in your heart. If it is in your heart to fly, fly. If it is in your heart to stand, stand. Anything but a denial of the truth. He that flies, has warrant to do so; he that stands, has warrant to do so. Yes, the same man may both fly and stand, as the call and working of God with his heart may be.[8]

Bunyan then gives examples from Scripture of people who at different times made the choice to "stand" or to "fly."

- Moses fled to Midian after he killed an Egyptian (Ex. 2:15), but he stood with the people of God when Pharaoh mistreated them (Heb. 11:24–26).
- David escaped when Saul sent his men to kill him (1 Sam. 19:12), but he stood when Saul came to a cave where David was hiding (1 Sam. 24:8).
- Paul escaped when his life was threatened (2 Cor. 11:33), but he stood when he went to Jerusalem, knowing that imprisonment and suffering were waiting for him there (Acts 20:22–23).

The same pattern is evident in the earthly life of Jesus, Bunyan notes. When the crowds were pressing in on Him, Christ withdrew (Luke 9:10), but when the mob came with swords and clubs to arrest Him, Christ stood and gave Himself into the hands of His enemies (Mark 14:43–50).

Having established this pattern from Scripture, Bunyan concludes: "There are therefore few rules in this case. The man himself is best able to judge *concerning his present strength, and what weight this or that argument has upon his heart* to stand or to fly."[9]

Look carefully at what he says. When it comes to deciding how to act in the face of opposition, we are in an area of Christian liberty. "There are . . . few rules." The person who is facing the opposition is in the best position to judge the right course of action, and they should do this by applying a "strength" test and a "heart" test. When you face opposition and need to decide if you should stay or you should go, you can discern the best course of action by taking note of your "present strength" and of the inclination of your heart as you consider the pros and cons of the decision that you face.

Applying the Strength Test and the Heart Test

Two examples, from entirely different worlds, will illustrate the application of Bunyan's wise counsel. One of my sons went through a period in high school when a particular teacher went way overboard in making barbed comments about his faith. I remember wondering what we should do. Should we complain? Should we change our son's schedule? After some reflection, Karen and I decided that we should wait and see what God would do, and in the months that followed, we saw our son grow as never before. He rose to the challenge and seemed to draw strength from it as his energy was focused on standing up to the teacher who had ridiculed his faith.

In this situation we observed, in Bunyan's words, our son's "present strength." If we had seen his spirit being crushed, we might have considered a different course of action, but God gave him strength to stand, and that was an indication to us that the right choice was to "stand" rather than to "fly." With regard to the heart test, at no time did our son ever ask or suggest that he wanted to step back from what he enjoyed. His heart was in what he was doing and this confirmed to us that standing was the path of wisdom.

In the years that have passed since these high school days, I have often found the strength test and the heart test to be useful. Take this and apply it to difficult choices you may face when you encounter opposition as a believer: What is your present strength? What factors carry the greatest weight in your heart?

A second (and very different) example also illustrates the application of these principles. Diane (not her real name), a daughter of missionary parents, was raised in Pakistan and early in her life sensed the call of God to serve the Afghan people. After studying in the United States, she returned to Pakistan in 1987 and began teaching English to Afghan refugees who were escaping from the war with Russia.

One day a letter addressed to Diane was handed to the security guard at the school where she was teaching. "I took the letter to the classroom," Diane told me, "and I can't describe the feeling that came to me as I opened it and read. It sent a jolt of fear through my entire body."

The letter said, in part, "Your school's teachers are publishing blasphemy amongst Muslim students, which is an unforgiveable crime. We know that you are not teachers and your aspiration is not just teaching English, but you are missionaries and your main aim is to spread blasphemy in Pakistan.

"We must let you know this is an Islamic country and you people do not have the right to spread your blasphemy material amongst Muslim students and encourage them to come to your religion. . . . This is our first and last warning; as soon as you get this letter you must close your blasphemy school, avoid having relationships with Muslims, and leave our country. Otherwise you will be responsible for our next action."

What would you do on receiving such a letter? Diane and her colleagues faced a painful and heart-wrenching decision. Would closing the school be a failure to trust in the Lord's protection? Would keeping it open mean signing a death warrant for the staff and the students?

"The school had been my life," Diane told me, "but I knew that I had to find my identity, not in the school, but in Christ. I had to realize that the school had been given twenty-seven years of fruitful ministry, and to accept that this was coming to a close."

Diane returned to America and, after a difficult year of transition, was surprised when a visa was granted for her to return to Pakistan. For a short time, she was able to work again among Afghan people, but more recently she was called into the Afghan embassy and shown a second letter from the Taliban, giving threats not only against her, but also against other women who were her friends.

Listening to Diane's story, it was clear to me that the wise decision she made to return again to the States reflected the strength test and the heart test that we have learned from John Bunyan. In this situation, Diane had to consider not only her own strength but also the situation of others, whose lives would have been put in danger by her continued presence. With her deep love for the Afghan people, she had to weigh differing arguments in her heart and, in the end, trust her disappointment into the sovereign hand of God.

In God's kindness, Diane has now settled in the Midwest, where she is actively engaged in ministry to a large and growing Afghan community. "I am so grateful to our wonderful Lord for protection," she says, "but more for His indescribable peace that washed over me time and again along the way at junctures in my life."

If you are persecuted in one place, Christ gives you liberty to move to another. "A man," in Bunyan's words, "is not bound by the law of the Lord, to put himself into the mouth of the enemy."[10] Sometimes it is right to stay and sometimes it is right to go, and the way you know the difference is by judging your present strength and weighing what arguments prevail in your heart.

GREAT BLESSING AND GREAT REWARD

The Setting: Places of Greatest Difficulty

Great blessing and great reward are often found in the places of greatest difficulty. Our Lord pronounces those who are persecuted and reviled as "blessed," and says that their reward will be great.

This promise and experience of blessing in the face of mockery, ridicule, slander, and physical persecution runs throughout the Bible. Peter says, "If you are insulted for the name of Christ, you are blessed, because the Spirit of glory and of God rests upon you" (1 Peter 4:14). Paul speaks of entering into "the fellowship of His sufferings" (Phil. 3:10 NASB), and when Shadrach, Meshach, and Abednego were thrown into the fire, the Son of God walked with them (Dan. 3).

Writing from prison, John Bunyan declared, "I have never in all my life had so much of the Word of God opened up so plainly to me before. Those Scriptures that I saw nothing particular in before have been made, in this place, to shine upon me. Also, Jesus Christ was never more real to me than now; here I have seen and felt him indeed. . . . I never knew before what it really was for God to stand beside me at all times. As soon as fears have presented themselves, so have supports and encouragements."[11]

Samuel Rutherford, a godly pastor who, like Bunyan, was imprisoned on account of his faith, speaks in similar terms: "I never knew by my nine years of preaching so much of Christ's love as He taught me in Aberdeen by six months' imprisonment."[12]

These men are saying that they knew more of the love of God and were given greater strength during the times of their trial than at any other time in their lives. You too will prove the promise of Jesus in this eighth beatitude as you experience the fellowship of Christ's sufferings, and so find blessing in the hardest places of your life.

The Outcome: Great Reward in Heaven

Along with great blessing, Christ also promises great reward to believers who are reviled, persecuted, maliciously slandered, and falsely accused. "Rejoice and be glad," our Lord says, "for your reward is great in heaven" (Matt. 5:12). "Reward" means that something will be given to people who suffer these evils that would not have been given otherwise. This principle is reflected in other Scriptures: Christ says, "Whoever gives one of these little ones even a cup of cold water because he is a disciple, truly, I say to you, he will by no means lose his reward" (Matt. 10:42). The reward here is linked specifically to giving a cup of cold water in the name of Christ. So something is gained by the person who gave the cold water that would not have been gained otherwise.

Our Lord told a parable in which three servants were each trusted with the same amount of money and were rewarded according to their stewardship. The servant who doubled his master's money was given authority over ten cities, and the servant who gained 50 percent on what was trusted to him was given authority over five cities (Luke 19:11–27). This parable suggests not only that God graciously rewards His redeemed people, but that He rewards us in different degrees, and that these rewards relate directly to our stewardship of what He has trusted to us in this world.

When Jesus says, "Lay up . . . treasures in heaven" (Matt. 6:20), He clearly conveys that we can have more there and less here, or that we can have more here and less there. Either way, what we do here makes a difference to what we have there.

Jonathan Edwards, the great American theologian, was convinced from the Scriptures that there are different degrees of happiness in heaven and different degrees of punishment in hell. "The glory of the saints above will be in some proportion to their eminency in holiness and good works here. Christ will reward all according to their works. . . . Christ tells us that he who gives a cup of cold water to a disciple . . . will in no way lose his reward. But this could not be true, if a person should have no greater reward for doing many good works than if he did but few."[13] Edwards then quotes other Scriptures that point in the same direction: "Whoever sows sparingly will also reap sparingly" and "One star differeth from another star in glory. So also [it will be] in the resurrection of the dead" (2 Cor. 9:6 NIV, 15:41 KJV).

But how can this be? If some have greater rewards than others, would this not lead to some being disappointed and living in heaven with regret that they had not done more? Edwards answers this with a marvelous image. Picture every Christian being like a clay pot, and imagine every pot being filled to the brim with water. The pots are different sizes, but each one of them is filled to its capacity. In the same way, every Christian will be a "vessel that is cast into a sea of happiness." Each of us will be filled to the brim with joy. Each will have as much joy as we can contain. More joy would not be imaginable or possible for us, and this will be true of every Christian. All of the pots will be full, but the pots will not be of the same size. "Every vessel that is cast into this ocean of happiness is full, though there are some vessels far larger than others."[14]

Edwards is not suggesting that we gain rewards in heaven like gaining frequent-flyer miles on a credit card. Even the best works of suffering Christians are shot through with our own sin and they are of eternal value only because they are sanctified in Christ. But the Scriptures give us this wonderful encouragement for the hardest times: "Blessed are you when others revile you and persecute you. . . . Rejoice and be glad, for your reward is great in heaven" (Matt. 5:11–12).

This eighth and final beatitude is surely the hardest calling for Christian believers. But great reward awaits those who suffer for the sake of the Savior, and Christ gives strength to suffering believers as we anticipate the joys that will soon be ours in His presence.

CONCLUSION

USE YOUR MOMENTUM

Years ago, while serving as a pastor in England, I heard John Piper make an extraordinary statement that I have never forgotten: "America is one of the hardest places in the world to be a Christian."

I remember thinking at the time, *that cannot possibly be true*, but having lived here for twenty years, I now understand what he was saying: the blessings of freedom lead us to expect a comfortable life, and comfort soon produces lethargy of spirit, which, in time, leads to fear and cowardice. The idol of comfort must be torn down and that happens through fasting, giving, serving, and risking, none of which is attractive to Christians whose primary goal is comfort and convenience.

Jesus said, "If anyone would come after me, let him deny himself and take up his cross and follow me" (Mark 8:34). "Anyone" includes every Christian. There are no exceptions to this calling. But the cost of following Christ will be unique to each individual. Each of us must take up his or her own cross.

When I think about the weight of the cross for brothers and sisters who suffer the harshest persecution, and contrast the suffering they endure with the freedoms and comforts I enjoy, I am moved by the difference and am challenged by how to make the best use of these privileges. If God should allow us to live in unusual prosperity, peace, and freedom, surely we must use these gifts to stretch ourselves in costly obedience to Him.

If our brothers and sisters in other parts of the world have their goods and livelihoods taken by force, we can choose to release ours in sacrificial giving. If other believers are in prison and we are free, we can use our freedom to extend ourselves with joy and without complaint in the work of Christ's kingdom. If other Christians are exhausted with the pains of beatings and torture, we can surely press through the tiredness and discouragement we often feel and find renewed strength in Christ to continue serving Him.

We began this book with the aim of making progress in the Christian life, and we conclude by seeing how the end takes us back to the beginning. The challenge of overcoming the lethargy that so often holds us back from a wholehearted pursuit of all that Christ calls us to be brings us again to the place where we began our journey. We don't have what it takes. The spirit is willing but the flesh is weak, and our best intentions die the death of a thousand excuses.

Welcome to the first ring! Knowing your need, you become "poor in spirit" and are thrown back in fresh dependence on the Lord. You begin to see and to mourn the compromises of your past life and to submit yourself with meekness to the will of God even when it is difficult and costly.

When these roots are established in your life, they will produce a hunger and thirst for God and His righteousness. From this desire, God will bring the good fruit of a tender heart filled with compassion, mercy, and forgiveness, a pure heart that wills one thing and pursues holiness, and a peaceable heart that will make it possible for you to be a peacemaker in a divided and troubled world.

The first ring is within your reach. Grasp it firmly and swing!

NOTES

Introduction: Gaining Momentum

1. Thomas Watson, *The Beatitudes* (1660; repr., Edinburgh: Banner of Truth, 1971), 114.

2. *The Heidelberg Catechism*, Question 114 (1563; repr., Grand Rapids: Faith Alive Christian Resources, 1990), 63.

3. C. H. Spurgeon, *Spurgeon's Sermons on the Sermon on the Mount* (1873; repr., Grand Rapids: Zondervan, 1956), 10-11.

4. D. Martyn Lloyd-Jones, *Studies in the Sermon on the Mount* (Grand Rapids: Eerdmans, 1971), 48.

5. Alexander Maclaren, *The Gospel of St. Matthew*, vol. 1 (London: Hodder and Stoughton, 1892), 66.

6. Alexander Maclaren, *The Beatitudes: And Other Sermons* (1896; repr., London: Forgotten Books, 2013), 11.

7. Ibid., 32.

Chapter 1: I Bring Nothing: The Enigma of Empty-Handedness

1. Martyn Lloyd-Jones, *Studies in the Sermon on the Mount* (1959; repr., Grand Rapids: Eerdmans, 1984), 35-36.

2. Thomas Watson, *The Beatitudes* (1660; repr., Edinburgh: Banner of Truth, 1971), 47.

3. C. H. Spurgeon, *Spurgeon's Sermons on the Sermon on the Mount* (1873; repr., Grand Rapids: Zondervan, 1956), 16.

4. Watson, *The Beatitudes*, 43.

5. Ibid., 47.

6. A. W. Tozer, "Boasting or Belittling," in *Man, the Dwelling Place of God*, rev. ed., comp. Anita M. Bailey (1997; repr., Chicago: Moody, 2008), 76.

7. Ibid.

8. Spurgeon, *Spurgeon's Sermons on the Sermon on the Mount*, 15.

9. Alexander Maclaren, *The Beatitudes: And Other Sermons* (1896; repr., London: Forgotten Books, 2013), 4.

10. Andrew Murray, *Humility* (Fort Washington, PA: CLC, 1997), 9.

11. Ibid.

12. Watson, *The Beatitudes*, 44.

Chapter 2: I Take Ownership: The Power of Spiritual Mourning

1. C. H. Spurgeon, *The New Park Street Pulpit* (1861; repr., Grand Rapids: Zondervan, 1964), 401.

2. Robert Murray M'Cheyne, *Memoir and Remains* (1844; repr., London: Banner of Truth Trust, 1966), 293.

3. Andrew Bonar, *Diary and Life*, ed. Marjory Bonar (repr., Edinburgh: Banner of Truth, 1960), 5.

4. M'Cheyne, *Memoir*, 366, from a sermon on Proverbs 8:4.

5. C. H. Spurgeon, "Mistaken Notions about Repentance" (sermon, Metropolitan Tabernacle, Newington, April 20, 1879), http://www.spurgeongems.org/vols46-48/chs2743.pdf.

Chapter 3: I Give Up Control: The Freedom of Total Submission

1. Thomas Watson, *The Beatitudes* (1660; repr., Edinburgh: Banner of Truth, 1971), 115.

2. Alexander Maclaren, *The Beatitudes: And Other Sermons* (1896; repr., London: Forgotten Books, 2013), 15.

3. Matthew Henry, *The Quest for Meekness and Quietness of Spirit* (Grand Rapids: Eerdmans, 1955; repr., Eugene, OR: Wipf & Stock, 2007), 126.

4. Ibid., 126–27.

5. C. H. Spurgeon, "The Third Beatitude" (sermon, Metropolitan Tabernacle, Newington, December 11, 1873), http://www.ccel.org/ccel/spurgeon/sermons53.xlv.html.

6. Ibid.

7. Watson, *The Beatitudes*, 119.

8. Ibid., 106.

9. John Calvin, *Sermons on the Beatitudes* (Edinburgh: Banner of Truth, 2006), 38.

Chapter 4: I Long to Be Righteous: The Energy of Renewed Affections

1. A. W. Tozer, *The Pursuit of God* (Camp Hill, PA: Christian Publications, 1948; repr., Chicago: Moody, 2015), 22.

2. C. H. Spurgeon, from sermon 3157, "The Fourth Beatitude," 1873.

3. Alexander Maclaren, "Thirst and Satisfaction, http//www.biblestudytools.com/classics/alexander-maclaren-last-sheaves/thirst-and-satisfaction.html.

4. Tozer, *The Pursuit of God*, 17, 23.

5. A. W. Tozer, *The Size of the Soul*, comp. Harry Verploegh (Camp Hill, PA: Christian Publications, repr. Chicago: Moody, 2015), 38.

6. A. W. Tozer, *Leaning into the Wind* (Wheaton, IL: Creation House, 1984), 18.

7. Arthur Pink, *The Beatitudes* (repr., Memphis: Bottom of the Hill, 2011), 30.

8. Martyn Lloyd-Jones, *Studies in the Sermon on the Mount* (repr., Grand Rapids: Eerdmans, 1976), 70.

9. "Jesus, Thou Joy of Loving Hearts," by Bernard of Clairvaux, as quoted in Tozer, *The Pursuit of God*, 15.

10. Maclaren, "Thirst and Satisfaction."

11. Tozer, *The Pursuit of God*, 2.

Chapter 5. I Care about Others: The Joy of Complete Forgiveness

1. See also Nehemiah 9:7; Psalm 86:15; 103:8; 145:8; Joel 2:13; and Jonah 4:2.

2. Sinclair Ferguson, *The Sermon on the Mount* (Edinburgh: Banner of Truth, 1988), 31.

3. Warren Wiersbe (born May 16, 1929) pastored for twenty years, including ten years at The Moody Church in Chicago. He is best known for his "Be" series of commentaries for ordinary believers on individual books of the Bible.

4. C. H. Spurgeon, "The Fifth Beatitude," (sermon, Metropolitan Tabernacle, Newington, December 21, 1873), http://www.ccel.org/ccel/spurgeon/sermons 55.xxxiv.html.

5. Thomas Watson, *The Beatitudes* (1660; repr., Edinburg: Banner of Truth, 1971), 149–50.

6. As cited in ibid., 144.

7. Lewis Smedes, *The Art of Forgiving* (New York: Ballantine, 1997), 85.

Chapter 6: I Go after One Thing: The Focus of Single-Mindedness

1. Thomas Watson, *The Beatitudes* (1660; repr., Edinburgh: Banner of Truth, 1971), 171.

2. John Bunyan, *Pilgrim's Progress* (Wheaton, IL: Crossway, 2009), 142.

3. Cited in James Black, *The Christian Life: An Exposition of Bunyan's Pilgrim's Progress*, vol. 2 (London: James Nesbitt & Co., 1875), 182.

4. J. C. Ryle, *Holiness* (repr., Chicago: Moody, 2010), 71.

5. The rich young ruler wanted to justify himself by keeping the Ten Commandments, and found that he could not do it (Luke 18:18–30).

6. Watson, *The Beatitudes*, 195.

7. John Owen, *The Works of John Owen*, vol. 3, ed. William H. Gould (repr., London: Banner of Truth Trust, 1965), 545.

Chapter 7: I Give Up My Rights: The Gift of Making Peace

1. Jesus pronounces eight beatitudes in Matthew 5:3–12. But the last of these (presented in chapter 8) describes the outcome of a godly life: persecution in the present world. Christians are not called to pursue persecution as we are called to pursue being poor in spirit, mourning our sins, meekness, hunger for righteousness, mercy, purity, and peace. But we are to expect that persecution will be the unavoidable outcome of pursuing such a life.

2. Thomas Watson, *The Beatitudes* (1660; repr., Edinburgh: Banner of Truth, 1971), 209.

3. D. Martyn Lloyd-Jones, *Studies in the Sermon on the Mount* (Grand Rapids: Eerdmans, 1984), 108.

4. Bishop Handley Moule, *Thoughts on Christian Sanctity* (London: Seeley & Co., 1888, repr., Eugene, OR: Wipf & Stock, 2007).

5. Ibid., 9.

6. Ibid., 12–13.

7. Ibid., 16.

8. Robert Murray M'Cheyne, *Memoir and Remains* (1844; repr., London: Banner of Truth Trust, 1966), 159.

9. Moule, *Thoughts*, 16.

10. Kent Hughes, *The Sermon on the Mount* (Wheaton, IL: Crossway, 2001), 63.

11. Robert Kennedy, *Thirteen Days: A Memoir of the Cuban Missile Crisis* (New York: Norton, 1999), 98.

12. Ibid.

Chapter 8. I Endure the Cost: The Price and Reward of a Godly Life

1. Open Doors website: https://www.opendoorsusa.org/christian-persecution/ cited in the web article, "Christian Persecution," (quick facts), August 3, 2014, by the Ethics & Religious Liberty Commission of the Southern Baptist Convention.

2. Ajith Fernando in William D. Taylor, *Sorrow and Blood: Christian Mission in Contexts of Suffering, Persecution and Martyrdom* (Pasadena, CA: William Carey Library, 2012), xxii.

3. Peter Marshall, from a prayer delivered to Congress on March 12, 1948, *United States Congressional serial set, issue 11305* (Washington, D.C.: Government Printing Office, 1949), 50.

4. John Bunyan, *Grace Abounding to the Chief of Sinners: The Spiritual Autobiography of John Bunyan* (Chicago: Moody, 1959), 109.

5. George Offor, "Memoir of John Bunyan," in *The Complete Works of John Bunyan*, vol. 1 (Grand Rapids: Baker, 1997), lxii.

6. Ibid.

7. Bunyan, *Grace Abounding*, 112, 113.

8. John Bunyan, *Seasonable Counsel, or Advice to Sufferers* (1875), reprinted as *Seasonable Counsel to Sufferers*, in *The Works of John Bunyan*, vol. 2 (Grand Rapids: Baker, 1977), 726.

9. Ibid., 726; italics added.

10. Ibid., 174.

11. Bunyan, *Grace Abounding*, 110–11.

12. As quoted in Kent Hughes, *The Sermon on the Mount* (Wheaton, IL: Crossway, 2001), 70.

13. Jonathan Edwards, *The Works of Jonathan Edwards,* vol. 2 (Edinburgh: Banner of Truth, 1974), 902.

14. Ibid.

ACKNOWLEDGMENTS

I would like to express heartfelt thanks to the many friends and colleagues with whom it is my joy to serve and without whom this book would not have been written.

First among them is Tim Augustyn, who prepared a first draft of these chapters from a series of my sermons preached at The Orchard. I reworked the material extensively and was helped in that process by transcripts of these sermons prepared by my gifted and godly assistant, Sandy Williams. Later, I had the joy of extended sessions with Tim in which we read through the evolving manuscript together making further changes and corrections. It is always a joy to collaborate with Tim and I am profoundly grateful for his gifts and for his ministry.

Tim serves with Unlocking the Bible, and our entire team—John Aiello, Margo Bott, Robb Hansen, Steve Hiller, Gina O'Brien, Lauren Rushiti, Annie Sander, Charlotte Speweik, Deb Weaks, and Kristen Wetherell—have all been encouragers and cheerleaders throughout this project. Thanks especially to Gina O'Brien, who first had the vision for this material being used as a small-group study.

My special thanks to Andrew Wolgemuth and Robert Wolgemuth of Wolgemuth and Associates, who facilitated the conversation with Moody Publishers that led to this book, and opened the door with LifeWay for the small-group curriculum.

Sincere thanks to all of the team at Moody with whom it has again been my joy to work. Jim Vincent made significant improvements to the manuscript, and Duane Sherman acted as liaison between the Moody and Unlocking the Bible teams.

I continue to be deeply thankful to the board and congregation of The Orchard Evangelical Free Church, with whom I have now enjoyed the blessing of serving for twenty years. Insights from members of our congregation are spread throughout this book. In particular, I am grateful to Skip Lundgren, who introduced me to "Diane," and to "Diane" for permission to share her remarkable story.

Finally, it is hard to imagine writing, preaching, or living without the love, patience, and support of my wife, Karen, who has listened to every word of this book read aloud at various stages in the process of writing, and has contributed greatly to it.

The boundary lines have fallen for me in pleasant places;
surely I have a delightful inheritance.
—Psalm 16:6 NIV

Can the Ten Commandments help you finally break through?

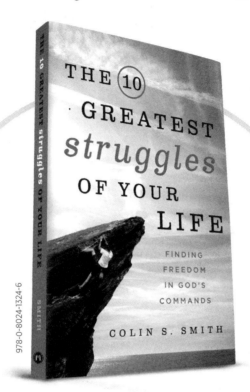

Do you struggle with busyness? With a temper? With dishonesty or discontentment? Whatever it is, find help where it may surprise you: the Ten Commandments.

In *The 10 Greatest Struggles of Your Life*, Pastor Colin Smith opens up the Ten Commandments to show how there is more to them than meets the eye. Moving from do's and don'ts to matters of the heart, they become barometers of your love for God. You'll discover areas of your life that are out of sync with His will, and you'll receive wisdom for living with greater love, strength, and freedom in Christ.

ALSO AVAILABLE AS AN EBOOK

MOODY
Publishers

From the Word to Life

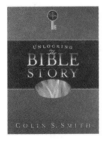
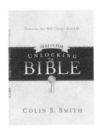

More from Colin Smith and Unlocking the Bible

Heaven, How I Got Here

What if you woke up one morning knowing that it was your last day on earth? That's what happened to the thief on the cross, who died a few feet from Jesus. *Heaven, How I Got Here* is his story, told in his own words, as he looks back from Heaven on the day that changed his eternity, and the faith that can change yours.

Book and Audio Book Bundle

Audio Book as read by Stephen Baldwin

Unlocking the Bible. With an audience of nearly 100,000, the program is now heard on more than 100 radio stations, via podcast and smartphone apps, and on the internet. The ministry challenges listeners to believe that their lives can be transformed by personal study of God's Word through 'the Power of the Open Book.'

Visit unlockingthebible.org or call us at 866-865-6253